"This great new book lays out some of the most dependable plants available for our gardens, in an clear, organized way. It takes the guess work out of gardening and will certainly help people be more successful in choosing what to grow!"

—Jessi Bloom, author of *Free-Range Chicken Gardens* and *Practical PermaCulture*

"No green thumb? No worries! Author and former editor of *Birds & Blooms* magazine Stacy Tornio guides you through the garden center like a good friend, pointing out the best of the bunch. With more than 100 easy, rewarding flowers, herbs, trees, shrubs, veggies, and even houseplants to choose from, you'll soon be on your way to filling your yard with beauty, your home with greenery, and your table with homegrown goodness. Stacy's lively, down-to-earth writing will keep you going back for more as you grow into a confident gardener with *Plants You Can't Kill*."

—Sally Roth, author of *The Backyard Bird Feeder's Bible*

"Stacy's many years of gardening experience translates into a book that makes it super easy to learn about great hard-to-kill plants. Each plant entry has beautiful photography, easy-to-follow tips and insider information that progresses from annuals through perennials all the way to herbs and vegetables. It's like having a knowledgeable garden center employee at your fingertips 24/7. This is a great gardening book for beginners or anyone afraid of failure. Remember, it's okay to fail, just try again!"

—Diane Blazek, executive director,
All-America Selections and National Garden Bureau

"In her many years of talking with readers of *Birds & Blooms* magazine, Stacy learned that fear of failure is one of the biggest obstacles to getting more people to garden. Her book addresses that head on by presenting beautiful, reliable plants in a simple-yet-effective way that anyone can understand, regardless of their experience level. It would make a great gift for any beginner gardener in your life."

—Susan Martin, perennial plant expert

PLANTS THAT CAN KILL

Also by Stacy Tornio:

The Secret Lives of Animals

The Truth About Nature

The Kids' Outdoor Adventure Book

We Love Nature!

Project Garden

Cathy's Animal Garden

Plants You Can't Kill

PLANTS THAT CAN KILL

101 TOXIC
SPECIES TO MAKE YOU THINK TWICE

STACY TORNIO

Skyhorse Publishing

Skyhorse Publishing books may be purchased in bulk at special discounts for sales promotion, corporate gifts, fund-raising, or educational purposes. Special editions can also be created to specifications. For details, contact the Special Sales Department, Skyhorse Publishing, 307 West 36th Street, 11th Floor, New York, NY 10018 or info@skyhorsepublishing.com.

Skyhorse® and Skyhorse Publishing® are registered trademarks of Skyhorse Publishing, Inc.®, a Delaware corporation.

Visit our website at www.skyhorsepublishing.com.

10 9 8 7 6 5

Library of Congress Cataloging-in-Publication Data

Names: Tornio, Stacy, author.
Title: Plants that can kill: 101 toxic species to make you think twice / Stacy Tornio.
Description: New York, NY: Skyhorse Publishing, [2017] | Includes index.
Identifiers: LCCN 2017014101 (print) | LCCN 2017018528 (ebook) | ISBN 9781510726796 (ebook) | ISBN 9781510726789 (pbk.)
Subjects: LCSH: Poisonous plants.
Classification: LCC QK100.A1 (ebook) | LCC QK100.A1 T67 2017 (print) | DDC 581.6/59—dc23
LC record available at https://lccn.loc.gov/2017014101

Cover design by Jen Ruetz

Printed in China

To my favorite redhead, Heather.
Thanks for teaching me about writing, gardening, and plant #71.

DISCLAIMER

No one associated with this book can be held responsible for you doing dumb or unwise things. This includes, but is not limited to, planting or consuming any of the plants in this book. It also includes encouraging others to plant or consume any of the plants in this book. I'd like to go on record right now to say that I DO NOT support eating, drinking, or absorbing any of these plants into your body any way whatsoever. And I absolutely can't be held responsible for your actions related to these plants. If you do have concerns or think you consumed something poisonous, seek medical attention immediately or call the American Association of Poison Control Centers at 1(800) 222-1222. Always plant responsibly. Gardening should be happy, y'all.

SPECIAL THANKS

This book wouldn't have happened without my lovely editor at Skyhorse, Nicole Frail. She came to me with the notion of the idea as a follow up to *Plants You Can't Kill*. We didn't know how, but we worked together to figure out the right approach to make this book a reality. I'd also like to thank my agent, Uwe Stender, who first took me on as a client with a book about gardening with kids. He's pretty much the greatest agent a writer could hope for. Please don't query him so he can spend all of his time on me. Finally, thanks to Denise Schreiber, author of *Eat Your Roses . . . Pansies, Lavender, and 49 Other Delicious Edible Flowers*. Denise knows what plants you can (and can't) eat, so she helped fact-check this book to make it editorially sound.

CONTENTS

START HERE!

If you do a search for poisonous or toxic plants, you'll likely be overwhelmed by the results. This is because there are a *lot* of plants out there that have some levels of toxicity, especially when it comes to affecting pets. No, not all the plants in here are going to kill humans, and this isn't the be-all-end-all guide to poisonous plants. But it's a good start to know which ones you should avoid. Check out the rating system below to help you know at a quick glance what kind of harm each one could cause.

LEVEL 1
A level 1 indicates a plant that is a nuisance but not necessarily deadly—unless consumed in large quantities. It will likely cause the most harm to pets, but keep an eye out for kids who like to explore with their hands and mouths.

LEVEL 2
A level 2 indicates a plant that could be harmful (to both pets or humans) in large quantities. You'll want to keep a close watch if you decide to grow any of these in your backyard.

LEVEL 3
A level 3 indicates a plant you want to stay away from. It likely has been linked to death (both humans and animals). Don't plant it in your backyard. It's not worth the risk.

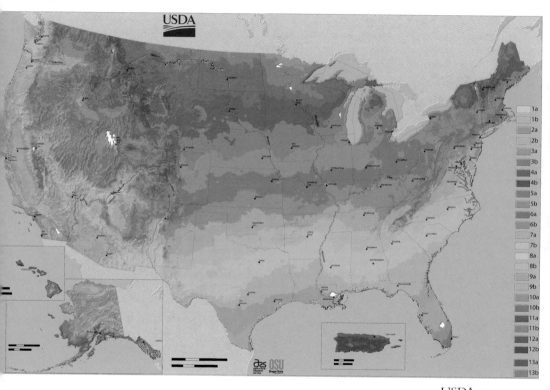

USDA

	1a
	1b
	2a
	2b
	3a
	3b
	4a
	4b
	5a
	5b
	6a
	6b
	7a
	7b
	8a
	8b
	9a
	9b
	10a
	10b
	11a
	11b
	12a
	12b
	13a
	13b

USDA.gov.

What's a Zone Map?

Most plants you buy (not annuals, though) will list recommended zones.
If you're unsure of your zone, check it on this map.

BULBS

"Live or die, but don't poison everything."
—Anne Sexton

DAFFODIL

Daffodils are some of the brightest and most cheerful flowers in the spring. They have great trumpet shapes, too. Every year, gardeners look forward to their blooming season because it's a sign that warmers days are ahead. Many gardeners like to plant daffodils in large groupings so dozens or even hundreds of flowers create a sea of sunshine. Most people don't realize that this plant has any poisonous qualities at all, but they exist in all stages of the plant.

DEADLY STATS

Common Name	Daffodil
Botanical Name	*Narcissus spp.*
Zone	4 to 8
Height	up to 3 feet
Spread	up to 2 feet
Flower Color	White, yellow, bicolor
Light Needs	Full sun to part shade
Level of Toxicity	1
Toxic Parts	All parts, including the bulb, contain a substance called lycorine.

☠ BE AWARE

If you, a child, or a pet eat any part of this plant, it can cause an upset stomach or vomiting. This usually passes after a few hours, but in a few instances, it can lead to more serious problems like damage of the liver.

GARDEN HISTORY

The botanical name of this plant has a great story. It was named after a very good-looking young man who admired himself excessively, so the gods turned him into a flower.

THE BOTTOM LINE

Plant it! Even though it can cause some mild irritations, this is still a good bulb to have in your garden. It's also one of the few plants deer won't eat, which is a bonus!

ELEPHANT'S EAR

POISONOUS PROFILE

This is one of the largest plants you can grow in your garden. It gets its name from its huge leaves—they look a lot like an elephant's ear! It can be sensitive to cold and might not make it if you leave it in the ground over winter, so it's only listed for zones 10 and 11. The trick around this is to dig it up in fall and save it to plant again the next year. That way, you can grow it just about anywhere.

DEADLY STATS

Common Name	Elephant's ear
Botanical Name	*Alocasia, Colocasia, Caladium, Xanthosoma*
Zone	10 to 11
Height	up to 6 feet
Spread	up to 6 feet
Foliage Color	Green, red, black, variegated, blue, multicolored, and more
Light Needs	Full sun to part shade
Level of Toxicity	1
Toxic Parts	All leaves and stems contain calcium oxalate, which grows more effective with chewing.

☠ BE AWARE

If you have pets that like to chew on big leaves, keep an eye out. This can cause drooling, pain, and pawing at the mouth.

THE BOTTOM LINE

This one is probably fine to plant, as long as you don't have pets that eat your garden.

CROCUS

Crocus are mighty plants quite popular with gardeners. These tiny blossoms, which are only a few inches tall, show up very early in spring. Many gardeners will just scatter these in throughout their lawn because they like random spots of color. Others will put them in containers, and then once they're done blooming, they fill the container with summer annuals. While this spring crocus can be somewhat poisonous, you'll also want to be on the lookout for the fall variety called *Colchicum autumnale.*

DEADLY STATS

Common Name	Crocus, Dutch crocus
Botanical Name	*Crocus vernus*
Zone	3 to 8
Height	up to 6 inches
Spread	up to 6 feet
Flower Color	Purple, white, variegated
Light Needs	Full sun to part shade
Level of Toxicity	2
Toxic Parts	All parts of this plant

BE AWARE

The spring crocus can cause an upset stomach, especially in pets. The autumn crocus is much more toxic and can result in kidney and liver damage and even death.

THE BOTTOM LINE

The spring crocus pictured here (the most common and blooms in spring) is probably okay to plant in your yard. However, it's best to avoid the autumn crocus.

HYACINTH

The next time you have a chance to look at a hyacinth, really take a close look at it. They have some of the most unique blooms when it comes to bulbs because they are made up of dozens and dozens of tiny, star-shaped blossoms. When you look at a photo, you might think that hyacinths are a lot bigger than they are, but they are actually just a few inches tall. Try growing them in the front of a garden bed so other plants emerging in spring don't overshadow them.

DEADLY STATS

Common Name	Hyacinth, common hyacinth
Botanical Name	*Hyacinthus orientalis*
Zone	4 to 8
Height	up to 1 foot
Spread	up to 6 inches
Flower Color	Blue, purple, pink, red, white
Light Needs	Full sun
Level of Toxicity	1
Toxic Parts	All parts are somewhat poisonous, but it's much more concentrated in the bulbs.

☠ BE AWARE

Pets are most at risk here, especially dogs. Poison occurs when dogs find a bag of the bulbs or they dig up freshly-planted bulbs from the garden. If they eat them, you might see signs of vomiting, drooling, etc. In extreme cases, it can affect their hearts.

▶ DID YOU KNOW? ▶

Another very popular type of hyacinth gardeners grow is called grape hyacinth. Many people think it's the same as the common hyacinth, but it's not. It even has a different botanical name, *Muscari armeniacum*. It's not toxic, though, so plant as much as you want without worry!

▶ THE BOTTOM LINE ▶

Plant away! Yes, you'll want to pay attention when you have bags of these out and are getting ready to plant in the fall. But once they're in the ground and the bulbs are put away, you shouldn't have to worry much.

STAR OF BETHLEHEM

POISONOUS PROFILE

You can put a few of these in the garden, and they'll quickly spread in just a few short years though they aren't really considered weedy by most gardeners. You'll also like this because its dozens of tiny little star-shaped white flowers can really light up your garden bed. However, in many areas, it is considered highly invasive and difficult to remove from the landscape.

DEADLY STATS

Common Name	Star of Bethlehem
Botanical Name	*Ornithogalum magnum*
Zone	5 to 8
Height	up to 1 foot
Spread	up to 1 foot
Flower Color	White
Light Needs	Full sun to part shade
Level of Toxicity	1
Toxic Parts	All parts can be poisonous, and even fresh-cut flowers can poison the water, making it toxic to pets, as well.

☠ BE AWARE

This plant has cardiac glycoside toxins, which affect the heart. For your cats and dogs, this can lead to vomiting, seizures, heart problems, and even death.

▶ THE BOTTOM LINE ▶

Plant it unless you have pets that like to graze on your garden. If so, then you probably want to skip it.

TRILLIUM

Since trillium is often seen in nature as a wildflower, most people don't even realize it's a bulb or that you can plant it in your backyard garden. If you go for a hike in the woods in mid- to late spring, then chances are you might see spots of trillium popping up all over. It's one of the few flowers that really thrives in the shade. You can find a few different trillium options to grow, including one of the most common with the botanical name *Trillium grandiflorum* or the red trillium called *Trillium erectum*.

DEADLY STATS

Common Name	Trillium, wake-robin
Botanical Name	*Trillium spp.*
Zone	4 to 8
Height	up to 1 foot
Spread	up to 1 foot
Flower Color	White, red
Light Needs	Part sun to full shade
Level of Toxicity	1
Toxic Parts	Roots and berries

BE AWARE

If eaten, the berries and roots of this plant can come with unpleasant side effects, like inflamed nasal areas and sneezing.

THE BOTTOM LINE

This is worth planting in the garden. You should look for it at native plant sales.

TULIP

POISONOUS PROFILE

One of the true signs of spring is when you see tulips pop up all across landscapes and gardens. If you want this to be the case in your yard, you'll have to plant them in fall because they need to spend the cold winter in the ground before they can bloom in spring. Dig a hole three to four times deeper than the bulb itself and drop it in, pointy side up. Make sure the base has good contact with the soil. You'll want to do this before the ground is frozen or too hard to dig. You can get tulips in any color you want (except blue), so happy shopping.

DEADLY STATS

Common Name	Tulip
Botanical Name	*Tulipa spp.*
Zone	3 to 8
Height	6 inches to 2 feet
Spread	up to 1 foot
Flower Color	All colors except blue
Light Needs	Full sun
Level of Toxicity	1
Toxic Parts	Most concentrated in the bulbs

BE AWARE

The toxicity of this plant is very similar to the hyacinth because they are in the same family. The bulbs are most toxic and can cause your pets to drool, vomit, or even experience heart and respiratory problems in extreme cases.

GREEN THUMB TIP

Many of the new tulip cultivars are gorgeous, but they don't last as long as the other varieties—some even just consider them annuals. Keep this in mind when planting. If you want a true perennial, talk to your garden center and ask them to recommend cultivars that will last for several years.

THE BOTTOM LINE

Grow this, but keep the bulbs out of sight of animals!

SNOWDROP

POISONOUS PROFILE

Occasionally blooming in January or February, this is truly one of the earliest blooming flowers you can have in the garden. Some people also call Star of Bethlehem by the name Snowdrop, but these are two different plants (check the botanical name to be sure). An old myth says that if you get only a single snowdrop in your yard then it's a bad omen. It's your choice whether to believe this, but to avoid it, plant several snowdrops.

DEADLY STATS

Common Name	Snowdrop
Botanical Name	*Galanthus nivalis*
Zone	3 to 7
Height	up to 1 foot
Spread	up to 6 inches
Flower Color	White
Light Needs	Full sun to part shade
Level of Toxicity	1
Toxic Parts	The entire plant is actually poisonous, but the bulb contains the most toxins. The bulbs can look a lot like onions, so don't make that mistake.

☠ BE AWARE

If the bulbs are consumed, symptoms might include dizziness, nausea, and vomiting.

THE BOTTOM LINE

This one is probably fine to plant. Since it's one of the first flowers to come up in late winter or early spring, it's a welcome sight in the garden.

AMARYLLIS

You probably recognize this flower because it's common to see during the holiday season. Stores will stock a version of this amaryllis along with pots to grow indoors as a houseplant, blooming right around Christmas. While this is definitely one way to grow this flower, it's not the only option. Those in warm areas can grow this flower outside year-round. Or you can grow it in the summer and dig up the bulb once the season is over.

DEADLY STATS

Common Name	Amaryllis
Botanical Name	*Hippeastrum*
Zone	8 to 10
Height	up to 2 feet
Spread	up to 1 foot
Flower Color	Red, pink, white, or a mix
Light Needs	Full sun to part shade
Level of Toxicity	1
Toxic Parts	Leaves, stem, and bulb

BE AWARE

While it's not as toxic as some other bulbs, it can still cause vomiting or a drop in blood pressure if consumed.

THE BOTTOM LINE

Go for it. It's a great garden bulb!

IRIS

POISONOUS PROFILE

So many different types of iris exist, including the one pictured here called Japanese iris (*Iris ensata*). Nearly all irises have poisonous qualities, so you'll want to be careful if you have pets that like to dig up bulbs or eat plants. However, they are pretty low on the toxicity level, so if you like these beautiful blooms, look for native species from your local garden center or at a native plant sale to find good options for your backyard.

DEADLY STATS

Common Name	Iris
Botanical Name	*Iris*
Zone	4 to 9
Height	up to 4 feet
Spread	up to 2 feet
Flower Color	Blue, purple, violet-red, pink, white
Light Needs	Full sun to part shade
Level of Toxicity	1
Toxic Parts	Most concentrated in the bulb

BE AWARE

The bulb of this plant can cause skin irritation, so you might want to plant with gloves. If an animal gets hold of the bulb, it might cause drooling, vomiting, or other irritation.

GARDEN HISTORY

The plant was named after the Greek goddess of the rainbow.

THE BOTTOM LINE

Plant it, but wear gloves while handling the bulbs. Iris are beautiful and will last for years, so they are a great addition to the garden.

CALADIUM

Caladium is actually closely related to elephant's ear—it even shares part of the botanical name—but it's worth knowing about it separately because you'll often see this sold at the garden centers as an annual. Like elephant's ear, most parts of this plant can cause problems for animals if they eat it. The bulb itself would likely cause the most harm. Other than that, it's a gorgeous plant, and gardeners love it for adding colorful foliage to their containers.

DEADLY STATS

Common Name	Caladium, Angel wings
Botanical Name	*Caladium bicolor*
Zone	9 to 10
Height	up to 3 feet
Spread	up to 3 feet
Foliage	Often bi-colors like green and white, pink and white, etc.
Light Needs	Full sun to part shade
Level of Toxicity	1
Toxic Parts	All leaves and stem and bulb

BE AWARE

The bulbs, which pets might come across and want to eat, are likely to cause vomiting and nausea. If you buy these as annuals at your local garden center, you probably won't have to worry, but keep this in mind, especially if you have any pets that like to dig.

THE BOTTOM LINE

They are good plants and have incredible color. Plus, so many cool varieties come out each year. So plant it!

SHRUBS

"All things are poisons, for there is nothing without poisonous qualities. It is only the dose which makes a thing poison."
—Paracelsus

OLEANDER

POISONOUS PROFILE

Oleander is one of the most deceiving plants out there. Home gardeners have been growing it for years—they love this small shrub for its beautiful blooms. Plus, it's relatively easy and fast to grow. But consider this your word of warning because oleander is one of the most deadly and toxic plants around. Consuming any part of this shrub—the leaves, bark, flowers, sap—can result in some pretty serious consequences or even death. Some areas of the country even consider it invasive, so this is one that you definitely plant at your own risk.

DEADLY STATS

Common Name	Oleander, Rose Bay
Botanical Name	*Nerium oleander*
Zone	3 to 9
Height	2 to 5 feet
Spread	up to 1 foot
Flower Color	Pink, white
Light Needs	Full sun
Level of Toxicity	3
Toxic Parts	All parts of the plant can do you harm.

☠ BE AWARE

Some of the toxic elements in oleander include cardiac glycosides, saponins, digitoxigenin, oleandrin, oleondroside, and nerioside. These can cause vomiting, dizziness, vision problems, and other issues like death. Stay away!

THE BOTTOM LINE

Don't plant it. It's not worth the risk to you or others with the whole "could cause death" and being invasive thing.

HEAVENLY BAMBOO

POISONOUS PROFILE

Gardeners love this plant because once you really get it established in the garden, it can have beautiful fruit (and plenty of it). Also, it has stems that look a lot like bamboo canes. It should be noted that this shrub isn't a native plant, and it's considered invasive in some parts of the United States, especially in the South. While non-natives aren't always a problem, this one actually can be. In fact, experts say many bird species are dying from eating these berries.

DEADLY STATS

Common Name	Heavenly bamboo, sacred bamboo
Botanical Name	*Nandina domestica*
Zone	6 to 9
Height	up to 8 feet
Spread	up to 4 feet
Flower Color	White with yellow parts
Light Needs	Full sun to part shade
Level of Toxicity	2
Toxic Parts	Berries

☠ BE AWARE

The berries of this plant are actually highly toxic. They could cause vomiting, upset stomach, and respiratory problems. Consuming a lot of berries can definitely lead to death in animals.

▶ THE BOTTOM LINE ▶

Don't plant this one. Instead, find a different native shrub to put in your yard.

ST. JOHN'S WORT

POISONOUS PROFILE

If St. John's Wort sounds familiar, then it's probably because you've seen it in the vitamin or natural remedies aisles of health food stores. It seems weird that a plant used to help us can also be viewed as poisonous, right? There are both native and non-native species of this plant, so inquire at your local garden center for more information.

DEADLY STATS

Common Name	St. John's Wort
Botanical Name	*Hypericum perforatum*
Zone	3 to 8
Height	up to 3 feet
Spread	up to 2 feet
Flower Color	Yellow
Light Needs	Full sun to part shade
Level of Toxicity	1
Toxic Parts	All parts

BE AWARE

It's usually not a problem, but in some instances where you have grazing animals in pastures, they will eat this shrub.

⟩ THE BOTTOM LINE ⟩

Unless you have grazing animals out and about near you, this plant is perfectly fine to grow in most backyards. It can be a bit aggressive and undesirable to a lot of gardeners, though. So there are probably better options (like forsythia) if the main thing you want is the yellow blooms.

AZALEA

You can find dozens upon dozens of azaleas to choose from both online and at your local garden center. They are some of the most popular shrubs for backyard gardens, especially in warmer climates. Not everyone realizes it, but azaleas are also known as rhododendrons, which relates to their botanical name. These plants produce beautiful spring flowers that come in a wide range of colors and shapes. Gardeners love azaleas because they reach their mature size in just a few short years, and then they are reliable bloomers for many more years in the future.

DEADLY STATS

Common Name	Azalea, rhododendron
Botanical Name	*Rhododendron*
Zone	5 to 9
Height	up to 5 feet or more
Spread	up to 4 feet or more
Flower Color	Pink, yellow, white, orange, red, purple
Light Needs	Part sun to part shade
Level of Toxicity	2
Toxic Parts	All parts can cause problems.

BE AWARE

Don't let kids or pets eat the flowers, leaves, fruits, or seeds of this plant. Sometimes the flowers can be mistaken for honeysuckle, but they're not! Mild symptoms might include mouth irritation, nausea, and vomiting. However, large consumptions can be quite serious!

GREEN THUMB TIP

This shrub definitely enjoys some shade, so keep this in mind before you dig.

THE BOTTOM LINE

If you have curious kids or pets, it's probably best to avoid this one. Because it's so beautiful, it seems to make it that much more appealing. However, if you don't have kids or pets to worry about, pick your favorite cultivar. You'll find so many great options to choose from!

DAPHNE

This is one of the earliest blooming shrubs you can have in the garden, sometimes flowering as early as February. It's considered native to forests, and it does really well in moist, wooded areas where there's lots of shade. Once this shrub flowers, you'll see small fruits reach maturity in early summer. While these berries are good for birds, you definitely don't want any little hands getting hold of them.

DEADLY STATS

Common Name	Daphne, Mezereon
Botanical Name	*Daphne mezereum*
Zone	4 to 7
Height	3 to 5 feet
Spread	3 to 5 feet
Flower Color	Purplish pink
Light Needs	Full sun to part shade
Level of Toxicity	2
Toxic Parts	All parts contain an acid that is irritable, which is especially found in the sap and berries.

☠ BE AWARE

When pets consume daphne, it can lead to drooling, vomiting, mouth and stomach problems, coma, or even death.

GARDEN HISTORY

The name Daphne came from a Greek myth that says Daphne went to Aphrodite, wanting to be saved from another god, so she was turned into a tree.

THE BOTTOM LINE

If you have kids around, you probably want to avoid this one. With the sap and berries being highly toxic when consumed, it's not worth the risk.

HYDRANGEA

The world of hydrangeas is *huge*! You can choose from hundreds, and the botanical names can get a bit confusing. One of the most popular is the bigleaf hydrangea, which has two main groups: those with globe-shaped flowers (mopheads) and flattened flower heads (lacecaps). Both are beautiful, and once you get them established, they grow for years! Don't lose patience if you don't get yours going right away. Sometimes you just need to find the right location in your garden.

DEADLY STATS

Common Name	Hydrangea
Botanical Name	*Hydrangea macrophylla*
Zone	5 to 9
Height	up to 6 feet
Spread	up to 10 feet
Foliage	Green
Flower Color	Blue, pink, purple, red, white
Light Needs	Full sun to part shade
Level of Toxicity	1
Toxic Parts	All parts of the plant can have elements that break down to produce cyanide.

☠ BE AWARE

You (or a pet) would have to consume a large amount of hydrangea plants to notice any issues. These might include a very upset stomach and bowel issues.

GREEN THUMB TIP

In cold climates, the wind and frigid temperatures may take a toll on hydrangeas. To protect your investment, cover plants in winter with burlap or shredded leaves.

THE BOTTOM LINE

Because you'd have to consume such a large amount to be in any kind of danger, you're probably fine planting hydrangeas in your garden.

HOLLY

This is one of those plants that symbolizes Christmas, winter, and the holidays for many people. Holly is often used in tabletop displays because of its rich green leaves and bright red berries. While it can grow quite big, most people keep it trimmed back to a few feet tall and wide. It can be a bit prickly (the leaves), which usually keeps kids away from taste-testing the berries, but you should still keep an eye out if you have one around. By the way, birds love the berries in winter when food is scarce!

DEADLY STATS

Common Name	Holly, American holly
Botanical Name	*Ilex opaca spp.*
Zone	5 to 9
Height	up to 30 feet
Spread	up to 20 feet
Foliage	Waxy green leaves and bright red berries
Light Needs	Full sun to part shade
Level of Toxicity	2
Toxic Parts	Berries

☠ BE AWARE

All holly berries are poisonous. If a child or animal eats holly berries, you might witness vomiting, diarrhea, dehydration, and drowsiness. This can occur after just a few berries, so you definitely want to take precaution if you know there have been a few (or many) eaten.

⟩GREEN THUMB TIP⟩

This plant is called dioecious, which means male and female flowers are on different plants. This means you'll need both a male and female if you want to get the colorful berries.

⟩THE BOTTOM LINE⟩

If you totally adore the idea of this classic plant, go ahead and risk it.

BARBERRY

This is a popular shrub for gardeners because it's easy to grow and provides flowers in spring, great foliage in fall, and berries for birds. Some areas consider barberry a bit invasive, so you might want to check with your local garden center before planting it. Otherwise, this is one of those shrubs you can count on for years to come.

DEADLY STATS

Common Name	Barberry, Japanese barberry
Botanical Name	*Berberis thunbergii*
Zone	4 to 8
Height	up to 6 feet
Spread	up to 7 feet
Foliage	Known for its rich burgundy leaves in fall and berries that are great for the birds.
Light Needs	Full sun
Level of Toxicity	1
Toxic Parts	All parts are somewhat toxic.

☠ BE AWARE

If taken in high doses, it can become toxic, leading to lethargy, vomiting, and even inflammation of the kidneys.

❯THE BOTTOM LINE❯

Don't be eating barberry raw or straight out of the garden. If you take it in pill form, just make sure you follow the directions.

ELDERBERRY

Trying to understand this shrub's toxic elements can get a little tricky because many gardeners see it as a wonderful shrub for the garden. It offers year-round appeal. In addition, the ripe berries can be made into jam or even fruit wine. However, if the berries are green or you eat some of the leaves, your stomach would not agree. If you're thinking about adding this to your yard, be sure to look for it by the botanical name *Sambucus nigra* and plant it in a sunny spot because it loves sunshine!

DEADLY STATS

Common Name	Elderberry, American elderberry
Botanical Name	*Sambucus nigra*
Zone	3 to 9
Height	up to 10 feet
Spread	up to 10 feet
Flower Color	White
Light Needs	Full sun
Level of Toxicity	1
Toxic Parts	Leaves, stems, and green berries

 BE AWARE

If you eat parts of this plant or the berries when they're green, you'll likely experience nausea, diarrhea, and in extreme cases, a coma.

> THE BOTTOM LINE

Leave those berries alone until they're completely ripe and are a dark purple or black color.

CHOKECHERRY

POISONOUS PROFILE

This is a plant that could be classified as both a tree or shrub, depending on the variety you have and then how you prune it. Chokecherries are generally great shrubs to have in your garden. They're native to the United States, and they produce edible fruits that many use for jams, jellies, pies, and more. (Well, that's if the birds don't eat them all first.)

DEADLY STATS

Common Name	Chokecherry
Botanical Name	*Prunus virginiana*
Zone	2 to 7
Height	up to 30 feet
Spread	up to 20 feet
Flower Color	White
Light Needs	Full sun to part shade
Level of Toxicity	1
Toxic Parts	Leaves, stems

☠ BE AWARE

This plant is a threat to livestock animals like sheep, cows, and other grazers that might come upon it in the pasture.

❯ THE BOTTOM LINE ❯

Plant it! There are so many good options and new cultivars around that chokecherry poses little threat to most backyard gardeners.

WITCH HAZEL

You don't come across many shrubs that bloom in the fall, but this is one of them. This plant has bright and beautiful yellow blooms that look like little ribbons along the branches. Many people know the witch hazel name because they see it in health food stores. It's often used on skin for inflammation or even acne as a natural remedy. While the toxicity of this plant is fairly low, it's still one you want to watch out for if you have pets.

DEADLY STATS

Common Name	Witch hazel, common witch hazel
Botanical Name	*Hamamelis virginiana*
Zone	3 to 8
Height	up to 20 feet
Spread	up to 20 feet
Flower Color	Yellow
Light Needs	Full sun to part shade
Level of Toxicity	1
Toxic Parts	Bark and leaves

BE AWARE

While it has a lot of benefits, especially applied topically, it can be toxic to dogs if they eat the plant out of your garden or if they get hold of it in pill form.

THE BOTTOM LINE

Plant witch hazel! You'll love the yellow flowers that pop up in September and October.

SMOKE BUSH

POISONOUS PROFILE

While some people know this plant as smoke tree, it's actually considered a shrub by most gardeners. This shrub doesn't have much in the way of flowers, but in the summer, it has hairy stalks that turn a smokey pink or purplish color, which help give this plant its name. Many people think this is a type of flower, but it's actually not. It also has great fall color, with leaves that darken to yellow, orange, or a deep purplish red in the fall.

DEADLY STATS

Common Name	Smoke bush, smoke tree
Botanical Name	*Cotinus coggygria*
Zone	5 to 8
Height	up to 15 feet
Spread	up to 15 feet
Foliage	Beautiful leaves that darken in fall
Light Needs	Full sun
Level of Toxicity	1
Toxic Parts	All parts are slightly toxic.

BE AWARE

While it's not one of the most toxic plants you could have in your backyard, it could still make your pets sick if they like to munch on leaves or stems.

THE BOTTOM LINE

This one is okay to plant in your backyard. Plus, you'll love the cool display it puts on from summer through fall. It's very unique!

FALSE HEATHER

POISONOUS PROFILE

This shrub produces beautiful purple blooms in spring and throughout the summer. However, since it only thrives in zones 9 to 11, most people who want to grow this shrub will have to think of it as an annual. Gardeners definitely love it for its flowers. It's also pretty low maintenance and fairly drought tolerant. So if you need a "plant it and forget it" option for your backyard, this is it!

DEADLY STATS

Common Name	False heather, Mexican false heather, Hawaiian heather
Botanical Name	*Cuphea hyssopifolia*
Zone	9 to 11
Height	up to 2 feet
Spread	up to 3 feet
Flower Color	Lavender
Light Needs	Full sun
Level of Toxicity	1
Toxic Parts	All parts

BE AWARE

You probably won't come across false heather much unless you live in a warm climate, but all parts of this plant can cause overall sickness or nausea in pets.

❭ THE BOTTOM LINE ❭

You might have a hard time finding this one in your area, but if you do, you should feel free to plant it without much worry.

BOUGAINVILLEA

Definitely known and grown for its beautiful flowers, bougainvillea can get quite large if you just let it go. Instead, try to keep this plant contained by keeping it pruned. It does really well with pruning and trimming, which is great if you have a very specific or small space where you're trying to grow it. Since it only thrives in zones 9 to 11, you might have to grow it as an annual in other areas.

DEADLY STATS

Common Name	Bougainvillea
Botanical Name	*Bougainvillea*
Zone	9 to 11
Height	up to 40 feet
Spread	up to 40 feet
Flower Color	Purple, red, pink, and yellow
Light Needs	Full sun
Level of Toxicity	1
Toxic Parts	Any parts of the plant with sap

BE AWARE

Most experts consider bougainvillea to be only mildly toxic. The plant's sap is a bit irritable to the skin, and if eaten in large quantities by your pet, it can definitely cause problems. Watch out for the thorns, which can also contain the plant's sap.

THE BOTTOM LINE

The blooms are gorgeous! Go for it.

CANDYTUFT

If you need a plant that is drought tolerant, candytuft is a great option. It doesn't grow very tall, but it has beautiful white flowers that butterflies and other pollinators really like. Is this plant a perennial or a shrub? It's a little bit of both. Depending on where you live and the variety you grow, it could be considered either!

DEADLY STATS

Common Name	Candytuft
Botanical Name	*Iberis*
Zone	3 to 8
Height	up to 1 foot
Spread	up to 2 feet
Flower Color	White
Light Needs	Full sun to part shade
Level of Toxicity	1
Toxic Parts	All parts

☠ BE AWARE

With mild toxic elements, you want to keep it away from all animals and any human consumption. It could definitely cause some queasiness and vomiting.

▶ THE BOTTOM LINE ▶

Go ahead and plant it! It's a great option for pollinators, and it's relatively risk-free.

CAPE PLUMBAGO

POISONOUS PROFILE

If you saw plumbago growing in its native habitat of South Africa, it would be a lot bigger. However, in the United States, most people grow it in a container, so it stays small and manageable. In fact, keeping it in a container is quite popular because this way you can grow it outside in summer and bring it indoors as a houseplant in winter.

DEADLY STATS

Common Name	Cape leadwort, plumbago, Cape plumbago
Botanical Name	*Plumbago auriculata*
Zone	8 to 11
Height	up to 3 feet
Spread	up to 3 feet
Flower Color	Pale blue
Light Needs	Full sun to part shade
Level of Toxicity	1
Toxic Parts	All parts

☠ BE AWARE

All parts of this plant are considered toxic, so keep it away from pets. Also, be aware if you handle it directly while planting because it could cause some skin irritation.

▶ THE BOTTOM LINE ▶

Grow this for the beautiful blueish flowers, which are fairly unique in the gardening world.

YEW

Yews are one of the longest-living evergreens, and they are a staple in many backyards. You've probably seen a yew, even if you didn't know what it was. While the entire yew family (*Taxus*) is huge and includes both trees and shrubs, they are very common as backyard shrubs. Plus the berries can seem really appealing to young kids.

DEADLY STATS

Common Name	Yew
Botanical Name	*Taxus*
Zone	6 to 7
Height	shrubs usually up to 7 feet
Spread	up to 5 feet
Foliage	Evergreen foliage
Light Needs	Full sun to full shade
Level of Toxicity	3
Toxic Parts	All parts have poisonous elements, including the seeds within the red berries.

☠ BE AWARE

Yews (especially the evergreen needles) can cause some serious heart problems if consumed. If left undetected or untreated, it could lead to death.

⟩ THE BOTTOM LINE ⟩

While you definitely want to stay away from consuming this shrub, yews are great for adding year-round color to your yard. They're also relatively disease-free and easy to care for.

CAROLINA ALLSPICE

This shrub is a beauty in the backyard, producing deep red or burgundy flowers. Gardeners love it for its long blooming seasons (spring to midsummer) and because it's so easy to grow. It'll tolerate a lot of different soil conditions, and it'll also do well in both sun and shade. Many varieties will also produce wonderful, sweet-smelling flowers, so inquire at your local garden center if this is important to you!

DEADLY STATS

Common Name	Carolina allspice, allspice
Botanical Name	*Calycanthus floridus*
Zone	4 to 9
Height	up to 10 feet
Spread	up to 12 feet
Foliage	Green with deep burgundy blooms or pale yellow
Light Needs	Full sun to part shade
Level of Toxicity	1
Toxic Parts	All parts, especially seeds

BE AWARE

The seeds can be especially toxic, so stay away. This is most often a problem when it comes to pets or animals like goats that will graze or potentially eat a lot of the seeds. You might see convulsions or elevated blood pressure.

THE BOTTOM LINE

You should be able to grow it just fine, but keep the toxicity in mind, especially when the plants might be dropping seeds (usually fall or late into your growing season).

TREES

"I mean, I have the feeling that something in my mind is poisoning everything else."
—Vladimir Nabokov

OAK

Everyone should plant an oak tree in their lifetime. It's the kind of long-term investment that can live on for hundreds of years. You can find lots of oak options like the popular white oak and red oak. Not every oak tree will reach that height of 80 feet, but it does need ample space. In due time, it will provide wonderful shade for picnics, reading, and relaxation.

DEADLY STATS

Common Name	Oak
Botanical Name	*Quercus spp.*
Zone	3 to 9
Height	up to 80 feet
Spread	up to 80 feet
Foliage	Leaves start off pinkish then change to dark green and orange, red in fall
Light Needs	Full sun
Level of Toxicity	1
Toxic Parts	Leaves and acorns

☠ BE AWARE

If grazing animals like sheep, horses, and goats eat a lot of leaves or acorns from oaks, they could absorb toxins that might cause kidney damage.

❯THE BOTTOM LINE❯

Plant it but probably keep your horses and goats away from eating the dropped leaves and acorns.

STRYCHNINE TREE

Be grateful that this tree isn't native to North America; it's one of the most deadly trees in the world, so it's good that you can't easily get your hands on it. This tree contains one of the most famous and age-old forms of poisoning: strychnine. In fact, its history is rich with people using it for that purpose, especially in the nineteenth century. The deadliness comes from the seeds, found in the large ball-sized fruit.

DEADLY STATS

Common Name	Strychnine tree, poison nut
Botanical Name	*Strychnos nux-vomica*
Zone	Native to India and Southeast Asia
Height	up to 30 feet
Spread	up to 20 feet
Foliate	Green leaves and small white flowers
Light Needs	Full sun
Level of Toxicity	3
Toxic Parts	Seeds contain strychnine, which can be deadly to all.

☠ BE AWARE

You pretty much need to stay away from this one. There's a reason people used it to poison others.

▶THE BOTTOM LINE▶

No. Just no.

BLACK WALNUT

The black walnut can be a beautiful tree, and it doesn't really harm humans. However, it's not really popular among gardeners because it contains something called juglone, which can harm nearby plants. Sounds odd, right? A lot of people don't even realize this about black walnuts, but then sometimes they have trouble getting plants to grow under it.

DEADLY STATS

Common Name	Black walnut
Botanical Name	*Juglans nigra*
Zone	4 to 9
Height	up to 100 feet
Spread	up to 100 feet
Foliage	Green with yellowish-green flowers
Light Needs	Full sun
Level of Toxicity	1
Toxic Parts	Roots and the nuts (but only to some)

☠ BE AWARE

Researchers say that the only livestock affected by the shavings of this tree are horses. However, the roots can also contain something called juglone, which can harm nearby plants.

THE BOTTOM LINE

There are better backyard tree options out there, so skip this one.

HORSECHESTNUT

This can grow to be a huge tree, which is relatively harmless. However, the nuts of these plants, which are green and spiky, can actually do a lot of harm in the right circumstance. Beneath those spikes lies a form of poison. You might have to work pretty hard to get to the poison of this plant, but you should probably still keep away as much as possible.

DEADLY STATS

Common Name	Horsechestnut, horse chestnut
Botanical Name	*Aesculus hippocastanum*
Zone	3 to 8
Height	up to 75 feet
Spread	up to 65 feet
Foliage	Green with white blooms in spring
Light Needs	Full sun to part shade
Level of Toxicity	2
Toxic Parts	The nuts in raw form contain a type of poison called esculin.

BE AWARE

If you make it past the nuts and consume them raw, side effects can include nausea, vomiting, headaches, convulsions, and even respiratory failure. It could even lead to death.

THE BOTTOM LINE

There are other (and better) trees to grow instead.

MANCHINEEL

POISONOUS PROFILE

This is definitely one of the most poisonous plants in the world, and you can't really get your hands on it, which is a good thing. However, there could be a chance you'd come across it in Florida or other tropical areas, so it's good to be aware of it. The entire tree contains toxins that can lead to death. Even just touching the tree (where you could come into contact with the sap) or breathing the air close to it could cause irritation to your skin or lungs. The fruit can look tasty, but remember there's a reason that it also has the nickname "apple of death."

DEADLY STATS

Common Name	Manchineel, little apple of death
Botanical Name	*Hippomane mancinella*
Zone	Native in parts of Florida, Central America, and South America
Height	up to 50 feet
Spread	up to 50 feet
Foliage	Green with fruit that look a lot like green apples
Light Needs	Full sun to part shade
Level of Toxicity	3
Toxic Parts	All parts

BE AWARE

If you eat this fruit, there's a good chance you won't see another day. Even coming in contact with it can cause irritation, so stay as far away as possible.

▶ THE BOTTOM LINE ▶

Run in the other direction.

BUCKEYE

If you happen to pay attention to botanical names, you'll notice that this one shares part of its name with the horsechestnut. They are closely related, even though the common names are quite different. This plant is very popular in certain parts of the country (like Ohio for the Ohio Buckeyes).

DEADLY STATS

Common Name	Buckeye, Ohio buckeye
Botanical Name	*Aesculus glabra*
Zone	3 to 7
Height	up to 40 feet
Spread	up to 40 feet
Foliage	Green leaves, light yellowish white flowers in spring, and orange, red, and yellow leaves in fall
Light Needs	Full sun to part shade
Level of Toxicity	2
Toxic Parts	All parts, including seeds, leaves, and bark

BE AWARE

If ingested, you might see signs of depression, twitching, inflammation, and vomiting. Especially keep an eye on pets that might be in an area where the seeds might have dropped onto the ground.

THE BOTTOM LINE

You might want to reconsider it if you have pets that like to graze in the backyard.

BLACK LOCUST

You might be tempted to grow this tree when you see the beautiful flowers it produces in the spring, but just say no. While it's not the most toxic tree available, it does have some annoying habits that gardeners don't like. It produces lots of suckers, or little roots and off-shoots from the main tree. These can be a pretty big pain to deal with in your landscape.

DEADLY STATS

Common Name	Black locust
Botanical Name	*Robinia pseudoacacia*
Zone	3 to 8
Height	up to 50 feet
Spread	up to 35 feet
Foliage	Green leaves with gorgeous white spring flowers
Light Needs	Full sun
Level of Toxicity	1
Toxic Parts	All parts

BE AWARE

Any animal that eats parts of this tree could experience vomiting, nausea, and other problems. Kids could be harmed if they get hold of the bark and chew on it. Otherwise, most cases involve livestock eating the bark or the seeds.

THE BOTTOM LINE

Pick a different tree to grow in your backyard.

RUBBER TREE

Did you know rubber is a natural substance that comes from trees in the wild? It is! This plant is native to Asia, where rubber tree plantations are common. Trees in the wild can reach more than 100 feet, but on plantations, they usually only get to 20 or 30 feet. The way you extract the liquid, called latex, from this tree is similar to the way they tap maple trees for syrup here in the United States. They drill into the trunk of the tree and then collect the liquid that drips out. After twenty or thirty years, rubber trees don't really produce anymore, and they'll likely get cut down. But knowing about this tree is pretty cool, right? While it's only mildly toxic, think about all the things that have rubber in them!

DEADLY STATS

Common Name	Rubber tree, which is different than the houseplant of a similar name
Botanical Name	*Hevea brasiliensis*
Zone	Mostly found in Southeast Asia
Height	up to 100 feet in the wild
Spread	30 to 50 feet
Foliage	Green with tree seeds that are a mottled brown
Light Needs	Full sun to part shade
Level of Toxicity	1
Toxic Parts	All parts have toxic elements.

BE AWARE

You likely won't come in contact with this plant, but you might want to make sure you don't have an allergy to latex because it could cause irritation.

THE BOTTOM LINE

If you can find it (you probably can't), then sure. Go ahead and grow it.

HOUSEPLANTS

She cracked a smile. "So what's your poison?"
He sighed dramatically, and let the truth tumble
off his tongue. "Life."
"Ah," she said ruefully. "That'll kill you."
—Victoria Schwab, *This Savage Song*

ZZ PLANT

POISONOUS PROFILE

As far as houseplants go, this one is kind of a newcomer. Yep, it's only been around since the 1990s and is becoming fairly easy to find because it's been really popular among gardeners. It gets its name because of the double Zs in the botanical name. If you come across this plant, you might think it looks fake at first because the leaves are waxy and look so perfect. You don't need a lot of light to grow this one, either.

DEADLY STATS

Common Name	ZZ plant, eternity plant
Botanical Name	*Zamioculcas zamifolia*
Height	up to 4 feet
Spread	up to 3 feet
Foliage	Rich green, waxy leaves
Light Needs	Low light
Level of Toxicity	2
Toxic Parts	All parts are poisonous, and the leaves can even cause irritation.

☠ BE AWARE

Pets and kids who nibble on the leaves of this plant will experience an upset stomach and vomiting. The leaves can also irritate hands by causing a rash.

❯THE BOTTOM LINE❯

Not a good plant for a home with kids or pets. It could make a good option for offices, though, especially since it doesn't require a lot of water or light to keep alive.

POINSETTIA

This one's potential poisonousness might come as a shock, but don't get too worked up. Rumors in the past have said that kids have eaten and died from poinsettias, but you might want to check the source. This plant is just mildly toxic to pets, but it's not going to cause serious problems for the most part. It can cause contact dermatitis to sensitive individuals, though.

DEADLY STATS

Common Name	Poinsettia
Botanical Name	*Euphorbia pulcherrima*
Height	up to 2 feet
Spread	up to 2 feet
Foliage	Green, red, and now many other colors because greenhouses and growers will paint them!
Light Needs	Low
Level of Toxicity	1
Toxic Parts	All parts, but especially the bracts (which many people refer to as leaves)

 BE AWARE

If your pets consumed a large amount of poinsettias, they might be affected with vomiting or nausea, but they would have to have eaten quite a lot!

THE BOTTOM LINE

Don't stop your tradition of having a poinsettia during the holidays. This plant is probably fine for most homes.

POTHOS

POISONOUS PROFILE

This is a vining plant that truly grows anywhere. It's been around forever and often gets over-looked, but it's so versatile. Plus, you don't have to worry about it getting diseases or having to repot it often. This plant does really well in offices because it doesn't mind (even thrives) on fluorescent light. Keep in mind that devil's ivy is one of the common names for this plant, so proceed with a little bit of caution.

DEADLY STATS

Common Name	Pothos, golden pothos, devil's ivy
Botanical Name	*Epipremnum aureum*
Height	trails up to 8 feet
Spread	trails up to 8 feet
Foliage	Green, heart-shaped leaves
Light Needs	Medium
Level of Toxicity	2
Toxic Parts	All parts

BE AWARE

Consuming a little bit of this plant probably won't cause many problems, but in larger quantities, you could see issues like swelling, vomiting, and difficulty breathing. It could make humans quite sick and, in pets, it could lead to death.

THE BOTTOM LINE

If you have pets or small kids, pick a different houseplant.

PEACE LILY

This is one of the most popular plants to give as a gift, and it's also one of the easiest house-plants to grow. It is known for the white "blooms." (They look like flowers but aren't tech-nically flowers at all. Instead, they are called spathes.) The most common mistake with this plant is watering it too much, so take it easy. Remember that it's easy to add water, but it's a lot harder to take it away.

DEADLY STATS

Common Name	Peace lily
Botanical Name	*Spathiphyllum wallisii*
Height	up to 2 feet
Spread	up to 2 feet
Foliage	Shiny green with white spathes
Light Needs	Low to moderate
Level of Toxicity	1
Toxic Parts	All parts, but especially the roots

BE AWARE

Mostly a problem for dogs and cats. You might see vomiting, increased salivation, and diar-rhea if ingested.

THE BOTTOM LINE

This one is a spring tradition for many, and it's pretty safe to have in your home unless you have an animal that really likes to munch houseplants.

SNAKE PLANT

The name alone is reason enough to grow this classic houseplant—you'll have something to talk about with your friends when they come over! The most important thing to remember with a snake plant is make sure you grow it in the right sized pot. Don't put it in a giant container or confine it in something too small. You want it to be just right, giving it a little space to grow. Once it fills the pot, move one size up.

DEADLY STATS

Common Name	Snake plant, mother-in-law's tongue
Botanical Name	*Sansevieria trifasciata*
Height	up to 4 feet
Spread	up to 2 feet
Foliage	Green with stripes and patterns that resemble a snake's skin
Light Needs	Low
Level of Toxicity	1
Toxic Parts	All parts

BE AWARE

If your pet eats enough of it, this could cause nausea, vomiting, and diarrhea.

THE BOTTOM LINE

If you're really looking for an easy-to-grow houseplant, this is a good one. Try it!

DUMB CANE

A lot of people think dumb cane and snake plant are the same thing, but they're not. Notice the botanical names are different even if they look similar. This houseplant is native to the West Indies, and if it grows in the right conditions or in the wild, you might even get lucky and see it flower. It can get pretty big, so this is another one that you want to make sure you have growing in the right sized pot.

DEADLY STATS

Common Name	Dumb cane
Botanical Name	*Dieffenbachia amoena*
Height	up to 6 feet
Spread	up to 3 feet
Foliage	Large leaves with interesting patterns of green and yellow
Light Needs	Medium
Level of Toxicity	2
Toxic Parts	All parts, and the sap from the leaves can be irritating if you touch it

BE AWARE

If a child or pet eats this, it may numb their throat and vocal cords! It contains calcium oxalate crystals that cause swelling in the mouth and throat, possibly for a couple of weeks. The sap also irritates skin.

❯THE BOTTOM LINE❯

There are other, better houseplant options if you have small children or pets who nibble houseplants. Because of the irritation the sap can cause, it'd be better to skip this one.

ENGLISH IVY

Here's another vine that is a staple in the houseplant world. Actually, it's a staple in many gardens, too. It can reach crazy heights of 80 feet in an outdoor setting. Indoors, it can trail quite a bit, too, especially if it has something to grow up or around. Inside, it'll be looking for a lot of light. But if you take it outside, it can actually tolerate a lot of shade.

DEADLY STATS

Common Name	English ivy
Botanical Name	*Hedera helix*
Height	up to 10 feet
Spread	up to 10 feet
Foliage	Green
Light Needs	High
Level of Toxicity	2
Toxic Parts	All parts, including the vine, leaves, and berries

☠ BE AWARE

If ingested, humans or animals might experience difficulty breathing, convulsions, vomiting, and paralysis or coma in extreme cases! Outside, the plant could produce berries, too, so that's another thing to watch for.

▶ THE BOTTOM LINE

Plant it (inside or out) only if you know it's going to be mostly out of reach of kids and pets.

JERUSALEM CHERRY

POISONOUS PROFILE

This is one of the coolest houseplants you can have. Houseplants tend to be mostly green, but when you grow Jerusalem cherry, you also get these bright and colorful fruit, which look a lot like little tomatoes. You're not going to want to eat these, though. So the lesson here is look but don't eat!

DEADLY STATS

Common Name	Jerusalem cherry, winter cherry
Botanical Name	*Solanum pseudocapsicum*
Height	up to 2 feet
Spread	up to 2 feet
Foliage	Rich green foliage with red fruit
Light Needs	Low to medium
Level of Toxicity	1
Toxic Parts	All parts, but concentrated in the fruit

☠ BE AWARE

While this plant isn't highly toxic or deadly, the fruits can still cause some nausea and upset stomach. Plus, because of its resemblance to cherry tomatoes, it might look like the kind of thing you want to eat. Just avoid, though!

❯THE BOTTOM LINE❯

Grow it as long as you don't have little kids around.

ROSARY PEA

The seeds of this plant are pretty popular for decorative purposes. For years, they've been used for jewelry like necklaces and bracelets. They are also popular in rosaries. There have been some disagreements about just how poisonous this plant or the seeds can be. However, a few deaths have been linked to it, so take that as a sign to avoid!

DEADLY STATS

Common Name	Rosary pea, jequirity bean
Botanical Name	*Abrus precatorius*
Height	up to 3 feet
Spread	up to 3 feet
Foliage	Green with bright-red seeds
Light Needs	Low to medium
Level of Toxicity	3
Toxic Parts	Especially the bright-red seeds

BE AWARE

It has high toxicity in the seeds, and if a person or an animal chews on the seeds, they may experience problems like vomiting, upset stomach, and even death in extreme cases.

THE BOTTOM LINE

Even though not all experts agree on the toxicity level, it's one you probably shouldn't have in your home, especially if you have kids or pets.

PHILODENDRON

This is a houseplant that has been popular for years. People frequently take cuttings of this plant and easily start new ones, passing them on from one house to the next. While it's not the most poisonous houseplant you can have, it's one that kids and pets often touch and get into because of its trailing nature. It can make a great and easy gift!

DEADLY STATS

Common Name	Philodendron
Botanical Name	*Philodendron*
Height	trails up to 6 feet
Spread	trails up to 6 feet
Foliage	Green with whitish or yellowish flecks throughout the leaves
Light Needs	Medium
Level of Toxicity	1
Toxic Parts	It has crystals of calcium oxalate called raphides throughout the entire plant.

BE AWARE

If a person or animal bites into parts of this plant, it releases toxic elements, and raphides will cause immediate reactions such as difficulty breathing and swallowing.

THE BOTTOM LINE

Skip this one. Since it can grow and be trailing, it's too easy for kids and animals to get at it.

ALOE

POISONOUS PROFILE

This one might surprise you. After all, doesn't aloe vera come from this plant? The answer is yes, but that doesn't mean it still can't be poisonous in other ways. There are a couple hundred different types of aloe out there, and they can vary a great deal in size and shape. The houseplant, aloe, is popular among gardeners because it's easy to care for and has beautiful, succulent leaves.

DEADLY STATS

Common Name	Aloe
Botanical Name	*Aloe spp.*
Height	up to 3 feet
Spread	up to 3 feet
Foliage	Thick, green leaves that get spiky in shape
Light Needs	Medium
Level of Toxicity	1
Toxic Parts	All parts have glycosides in them.

BE AWARE

If consumed, you'll likely experience vomiting and diarrhea. The side effects are generally mild, but keep an eye on any animal who might munch on this plant, especially if they've eaten a lot.

THE BOTTOM LINE

Yes! Aloe is a great houseplant for most.

BIRD-OF-PARADISE

POISONOUS PROFILE

If you go down to southern Florida or other tropical areas, you'll likely see this plant growing in the wild. It gets its name from the unique and colorful bloom shape, which tends to resemble a bird's bill. You really don't find a lot of similar blooms like it in the wild. It's so popular that you often see it available as a cut flower, too. It's definitely one of the most interesting houseplants you could have.

DEADLY STATS

Common Name	Bird-of-paradise
Botanical Name	*Strelitzia reginae*
Height	up to 4 feet
Spread	up to 4 feet
Foliage	Green with very distinct and unique orange and blue blooms
Light Needs	Medium
Level of Toxicity	1
Toxic Parts	All parts of the plant have a toxin, which is released when bitten.

BE AWARE

Dogs are most at risk with this plant. If you have one and they bite or chew it, then you might notice them drooling and staggering a bit. In extreme cases or if they've consumed a lot, it could be more serious.

❯THE BOTTOM LINE❯

Keep it out of reach of pets. This one is such a cool houseplant to have!

JADE PLANT

POISONOUS PROFILE

The jade plant has a bit of good superstition behind it. For years, people have been giving it as a gift because they believe it will bring the receiver wealth and good fortune. So it's a popular houseplant given for a new job, new home, etc. It also has an excellent reputation among gardeners as being really easy to care for. You don't have to water it much, so if you have a jade plant, you can feel confident you'll have it around for a few years. However, if you have pets at all, it might not be the best houseplant for you. Take a look.

DEADLY STATS

Common Name	Jade plant, money tree, lucky plant
Botanical Name	*Crassula ovata*
Height	up to 1 foot
Spread	up to 1 foot
Foliage	Beautiful green succulent-type leaves
Light Needs	Medium
Level of Toxicity	2
Toxic Parts	All parts, including the leaves, which are especially appealing to pets because of their small size

☠ BE AWARE

Vomiting, slow heart rate, and even depression are all symptoms that might come from consuming jade. If eaten in large quantities, it can definitely be deadly to pets.

❯THE BOTTOM LINE❯

Because of its small size, it might be easier and more appealing to pets, so it's best to skip it.

SAGO PALM

If you like the idea of having your very own palm tree, then this might be the houseplant you've always dreamed of. These plants get much, much bigger if grown in their native tropical environment. However, they've been cultivated to make great (and showy) houseplants. They are considered relatively easy to grow. Plus if you have a big space to fill, it can definitely do that!

DEADLY STATS

Common Name	Sago palm
Botanical Name	*Cycas revoluta*
Height	up to 3 feet
Spread	up to 3 feet
Foliage	Feathery green
Light Needs	Medium
Level of Toxicity	2
Toxic Parts	All parts

BE AWARE

This plant can cause serious damage to the liver of humans or animals that consume it, and it's been known to kill dogs who have eaten a lot of it. You might also experience vomiting, increased thirst, etc.

❯ THE BOTTOM LINE ❯

You should skip this plant, especially if you have pets that like to nibble. Since the needles easily drop off this plant, it makes it readily available for pets.

FICUS TREE

Love the idea of having your own miniature tree inside your home? The ficus tree is going to be one of your best bets! While all varieties of ficus are known to have a sap that can be irritating, it is still a very popular houseplant. If you have one, make sure it gets lots of moisture, and keep it in a warm area. It doesn't do too well in cold or drafty places in the house.

DEADLY STATS

Common Name	Ficus tree, weeping fig
Botanical Name	*Ficus benjamina*
Height	up to 4 feet
Spread	up to 2 feet
Foliage	Rich, glossy green leaves
Light Needs	Low
Level of Toxicity	1
Toxic Parts	All parts, especially the sap that can come out of bark, leaves, etc.

BE AWARE

If you get ficus sap on your skin, it might cause some irritation. If pets get hold of the leaves (which are known to drop) and eat them, this might cause them vomiting, diarrhea, and sickness.

THE BOTTOM LINE

It's probably fine for most homes, but be sure to watch for leaf drop, and then clean up right away.

WEEDS, WILDFLOWERS & VINES

"Now, a clever man would put the poison into his own goblet, because he would know that only a great fool would reach for what he was given. I am not a great fool, so I can clearly not choose the wine in front of you. But you must have known I was not a great fool, you would have counted on it, so I can clearly not choose the wine in front of me."
—Vizzini, *The Princess Bride*

53. Leopard's bane   91

54. Jimsonweed   92

55. Stinging nettle   93

56. Tansy mustard   95

57. Nightshade   96

58. Castor bean   97

59. Wisteria   99

60. Moonseed   100

61. Poison parsnip   101

62. Clematis   103

63. Bryonia   104

64. Mistletoe   105

65. Trumpet vine   107

66. Water hemlock   108

67. Monkshood   109

LEOPARD'S BANE

It's not native to the United States, but this doesn't stop it, with its yellow, daisy-like blooms, from being a popular flower among gardeners. You can find a few different species of leopard's bane under the botanical name of *Doronicum*. These plants are easy to grow in both sun and shade, which is why it's common to see them popping up along roadsides or in the wild.

DEADLY STATS

Common Name	Leopard's bane
Botanical Name	*Doronicum spp.*
Zone	4 to 9
Height	up to 3 feet
Spread	up to 2 feet
Flower Color	Yellow
Light Needs	Full sun to part shade
Level of Toxicity	2
Toxic Parts	All parts contain a toxin called helenalin.

☠ BE AWARE

If you touch this plant, it could irritate your skin. Otherwise, you might see signs of vomiting, shortness of breath, and heart palpitations.

THE BOTTOM LINE

Only plant it if you don't have to worry about kids or pets who might eat it. You'll also want to wear gloves when handling it.

JIMSONWEED

POISONOUS PROFILE

It wouldn't be uncommon to see this plant pop up in your yard, garden, or veggie bed. You might even be tempted to keep it growing because it looks relatively harmless. Plus, it eventually produces pretty purple flowers. But just say no to this one. It does have "weed" in its name for a reason. This plant can be invasive (and poisonous), so discourage it from growing wherever you can.

DEADLY STATS

Common Name	Jimsonweed, stinkweed, devil's apple
Botanical Name	*Datura stramonium*
Zone	3 to 9
Height	up to 4 feet
Spread	up to 4 feet
Flower Color	White or lavender
Light Needs	Full sun to part shade
Level of Toxicity	2
Toxic Parts	All parts, including the sap, which can cause skin rash

BE AWARE

Symptoms include hallucinations, convulsions, and even coma. While it takes a lot of this to cause real damage, even breathing in the fragrance of the flowers has been known to make people dizzy. Grazing animals like cattle and sheep can die from this if they eat a lot.

❭THE BOTTOM LINE❭

Skip this one. Don't encourage anyone to grow it. It is a weed after all!

STINGING NETTLE

Unfortunately, you've probably come into contact with stinging nettle. It pops up in the wild, in backyards, and anywhere else you do *not* want it to grow. It might not look that harmful at first glance, but if your skin comes into contact with it, you'll definitely know right away. It really does "sting" you, with the pain intensifying every second. Sure, this might seem like a pretty harmless plant overall, but it's not one you want in your garden. Some varieties of it (one in New Zealand in particular) are even known to cause death!

DEADLY STATS

Common Name	Stinging nettle
Botanical Name	*Urtica dioica*
Zone	3 to 9
Height	up to 7 feet
Spread	up to 3 feet
Flower Color	Yellow, white, purple, green
Light Needs	Full sun to part shade
Level of Toxicity	2
Toxic Parts	Tiny hairs on the leaves

BE AWARE

The little hairs on the leaves can break off and stick into the skin. When this happens, a little poison can enter, making it very painful to the recipient—both humans and animals.

THE BOTTOM LINE

Don't plant it, and don't go near it. It hurts!

TANSY MUSTARD

This flower/weed is common throughout the United States. You'll often see it growing along the side of the road or in meadows, but it's easy to miss since it only grows a few feet high. This plant with bright yellow blooms is related to the mustard family. You can recognize it because it blooms in early spring, and its leaves look a lot like ferns starting to grow.

DEADLY STATS

Common Name	Tansy mustard
Botanical Name	*Descurainia pinnata*
Zone	3 to 9
Height	up to 3 feet
Spread	up to 1 foot
Flower Color	Yellow
Light Needs	Full sun
Level of Toxicity	1
Toxic Parts	All parts, especially when the plant is small

☠ BE AWARE

Animals will experience symptoms of a paralyzed tongue, and if they eat enough of it, they could become blind.

⟩THE BOTTOM LINE⟩

Stay away from this one if you see it in the wild. Don't be drawn in by its cute, button-shaped, and curious-looking yellow blooms.

NIGHTSHADE

Many plants go by the name of nightshade, and you pretty much want to stay away from them all. The one pictured here is a vine with the most beautiful deep-purple flowers, but don't let them fool you. You don't want any part of it. Also keep an eye out for similar plants with this bloom shape or in this family. While some are more toxic than others, you pretty much want to avoid them.

DEADLY STATS

Common Name	Nightshade, bittersweet nightshade, climbing nightshade
Botanical Name	*Solanum dulcamara*
Zone	4 to 8
Height	up to 7 feet
Spread	up to 7 feet
Flower Color	Purple
Light Needs	Full sun to part shade
Level of Toxicity	3
Toxic Parts	All parts, which can cause irritation to the skin as well

BE AWARE

This is one of the more deadly plants you can find in the garden, and this one can especially be a problem because it grows fast and spreads quickly. If consumed, it can cause vomiting, upset stomach, and even death in serious cases and large quantities.

▶ THE BOTTOM LINE ◀

Find a different vine if you're looking for something to grow up that trellis.

CASTOR BEAN

POISONOUS PROFILE

This plant first gained popularity because it's huge and very striking. It can shoot up to 10 feet in a single growing season, and the little seed balls you find on the plant are red and spiky. However, it comes with a price. Those little seeds can really do some damage if consumed by people or pets. The plant can also cause irritation if you touch it or rub against it.

DEADLY STATS

Common Name	Castor bean
Botanical Name	*Ricinus communis*
Zone	9 to 11
Height	up to 10 feet
Spread	up to 4 feet
Flower Color	Small greenish-yellow flowers, though mostly known for the spiky red seed capsules
Light Needs	Full sun
Level of Toxicity	3
Toxic Parts	All, but the seeds are most dangerous

☠ BE AWARE

Nausea, vomiting, abdominal pain, respiratory problems, and even death can occur if consumed. Also, symptoms don't always show up right away.

▶ THE BOTTOM LINE ▶

It's aggressive, it's highly poisonous, and it's not worth it. Don't encourage it in your garden.

WISTERIA

POISONOUS PROFILE

Wisteria is one of the coveted plants that once you see it growing, you really want to have it yourself. It might take a couple years to get wisteria established, but once you do, it's so beautiful. It produces gorgeous spring blooms, year after year. This vine can get pretty huge, so keep this in mind if you plant it. You'll want to either grow it on a support system or have it in a place where you can add support once it's established.

DEADLY STATS

Common Name	Wisteria
Botanical Name	*Wisteria frutescens*
Zone	5 to 9
Height	up to 30 feet
Spread	up to 8 feet
Flower Color	Lilac or purple
Light Needs	Full sun
Level of Toxicity	1
Toxic Parts	All parts, especially the seeds and seed pods

BE AWARE

If your pet eats parts of this plant, you might notice signs of vomiting, diarrhea, and upset stomach. It can even cause pet depression!

THE BOTTOM LINE

This one is probably fine to grow in your garden. It often grows as a vine, so your pets might not even be able to reach it.

MOONSEED

This plant is a common vine across North America. While it's not one often grown in backyards, you will see it in the wild. In fact, it can look a lot like wild grapes, which is why it's so important to know what you're looking for if you go foraging. This plant spreads by rhizomes, so if it does get going in backyard gardens, it can be a bit aggressive.

DEADLY STATS

Common Name	Moonseed
Botanical Name	*Menispermum canadense*
Zone	5 to 8
Height	up to 20 feet
Spread	up to 6 feet
Flower Color	Greenfish-white flowers
Light Needs	Full sun to part shade
Level of Toxicity	3
Toxic Parts	All parts, especially leaves and fruit

☠ BE AWARE

The fruit on this plant looks a lot like grapes, and it can be fatal.

❯THE BOTTOM LINE❯

Do *not* confuse this plant with wild grapes. It can be tricky, but be sure you know what you're looking at.

POISON PARSNIP

POISONOUS PROFILE

Poison or wild parsnip is a bit of a sneaky plant. It looks a lot like a wildflower. However, if you come into contact with it, it could cause a serious burning and blistering of your skin within a short amount of time. This plant, considered a weed by many gardeners, is common in pastures, along roadsides, and other parts of the wild. It's important to know what it looks like and not confuse it with other look-alikes.

DEADLY STATS

Common Name	Poison parsnip, wild parsnip
Botanical Name	*Pastinaca sativa*
Zone	4 to 9
Height	up to 5 feet
Spread	up to 3 feet
Flower Color	Yellow
Light Needs	Full sun
Level of Toxicity	1
Toxic Parts	All parts

BE AWARE

It might not cause death, but it contains a substance that makes skin sensitive to light. If you handle this plant, it could cause mild to moderate skin irritations, which look a lot like burns or blisters.

❯ THE BOTTOM LINE ❯

Don't handle it at all. It's pretty weedy, so it's not a desirable plant overall.

CLEMATIS

Clematis is one of the most popular vines in the garden. There are many different types of clematis out there, and the beautiful flowers that this plant is known for come in many different shades. Clematis starts off small in the spring, but it doesn't take long for it to grow up a trellis or pergola. As a bonus, many gardeners are able to grow it in partial shade, making it a truly versatile bloom.

DEADLY STATS

Common Name	Clematis
Botanical Name	*Clematis*
Zone	5 to 9
Height	up to 10 feet
Spread	up to 6 feet
Flower Color	Blue, white, purple, pink, red
Light Needs	Full sun to part shade
Level of Toxicity	1
Toxic Parts	All parts

BE AWARE

Clematis can cause mouth pain to animals who eat it. Other side effects include vomiting, salivating, and diarrhea.

THE BOTTOM LINE

It's probably fine for most backyards and gardens, but keep it away from pets.

BRYONIA

Bryonia definitely falls into the weed category. While it's not native to the United States, a type of bryonia (white bryony) can be found in western parts of the United States like Washington, Montana, and Idaho. It's never a good idea to eat unknown berries in the wild, but you should definitely keep a watch out for this vining plant.

DEADLY STATS

Common Name	Bryonia, bryony
Botanical Name	*Bryonia*
Zone	Mostly native to parts of Europe and Southeast Asia
Height	20 feet or more
Spread	10 feet or more
Flower Color	A greenish-white flower
Light Needs	Full sun
Level of Toxicity	3
Toxic Parts	All parts, especially the berries

BE AWARE

If you consume any parts of this plant or the berries, you may experience nausea or vomiting. As little as 30 to 40 berries could cause death in humans or animals.

THE BOTTOM LINE

Skip it!

MISTLETOE

Many people don't know this, but mistletoe is actually a type of parasite. Seems weird, right? Isn't this just a holiday plant that encourages people to kiss? This is a plant that lives on trees, and it actually can do a lot of damage to the trees if left untreated. Mistletoe attaches to trees, and then it sucks away vital water and nutrients. If you don't do something to get rid of it, it can actually kill the tree.

DEADLY STATS

Common Name	Mistletoe
Botanical Name	*Phoradendron serotinum* and *Viscum album*
Zone	3 to 9
Height	Up to 5 feet
Spread	Up to 5 feet
Foliage	Green with small white berries
Light Needs	Sun to part shade
Level of Toxicity	1
Toxic Parts	All parts, but especially the berries

☠ BE AWARE

For humans, it's mostly the berries from mistletoe that you have to worry about. If you or even a pet consumes them, you could see side effects like vomiting and an upset stomach.

▶ THE BOTTOM LINE ◀

If you notice a tree with mistletoe in it (it's usually really high up), try to get help from an arborist. Remove the mistletoe, if possible.

TRUMPET VINE

Trumpet vine is one of the biggest, most striking, awesome hummingbird plants that you can grow. Once you get it established, it loyally comes back every year, growing 20, 30, and even 40 feet, attracting hummingbirds the entire season. The trumpet-shaped flowers are gorgeous and bright. They will also attract butterflies and bees. You definitely need a strong support system to grow this vine—an old stump, a sturdy pergola, even a telephone pole. It's truly one of the most eye-catching plants in the garden.

DEADLY STATS

Common Name	Trumpet vine, trumpet creeper
Botanical Name	*Campsis radicans*
Zone	4 to 9
Height	10 to 40 feet
Spread	5 to 20 feet
Flower Color	Orange, scarlet, or yellow
Light Needs	Full sun to part shade
Level of Toxicity	1
Toxic Parts	Leaves, flowers

BE AWARE

If you touch this plant, it could cause some minor skin irritation like redness. If consumed, mild effects include vomiting and nausea.

THE BOTTOM LINE

The toxic elements are pretty low, so this is one that you should feel okay about planting.

WATER HEMLOCK

You might know the name *hemlock* because of the tree, but this is in a completely different botanical family. You usually find it growing in the wild. It's especially common in wetland areas and around pastures and streams. It's one of the most deadly plants you can find in the wild, both to animals and humans. Some people often mistake it for parsnips or herbs, but if you see something like this plant growing, just let it be!

DEADLY STATS

Common Name	Water hemlock
Botanical Name	*Cicuta douglasii*
Zone	5 to 9
Height	up to 3 feet
Spread	up to 3 feet
Flower Color	Small white clusters of flowers
Light Needs	Part sun to part shade
Level of Toxicity	3
Toxic Parts	All parts, especially the roots

☠ BE AWARE

If consumed, especially the roots, this can cause serious seizures and convulsions. It can also lead to heart issues and even death.

❯ THE BOTTOM LINE ❯

If you come across this, leave it alone!

MONKSHOOD

This plant also goes by the common name of wolfsbane because parts of this plant were once used to poison wolves—both as a bait and also as a poison in the arrow. It has a long history of growing in the wild and being used for poisonous purposes, so you definitely don't want to consume it. However, it's still popular among gardeners, especially for its bluish blooms. They make a statement in the backyard!

DEADLY STATS

Common Name	Monkshood, wolfsbane
Botanical Name	*Aconitum napellus*
Zone	3 to 7
Height	up to 4 feet
Spread	up to 2 feet
Flower Color	Purplish blue flowers
Light Needs	Full sun to part shade
Level of Toxicity	3
Toxic Parts	All parts, but especially the roots and leaves

BE AWARE

If consumed, you'll see nausea and vomiting, along with burning, tingling, and numbness. You or your pet might also see difficulty breathing, dizziness, and serious heart problems, which can lead to death.

▶ THE BOTTOM LINE ◀

Don't plant it. It's been known to kill humans, too, and it's certainly not worth the risk.

PERENNIALS

"If you drink much from a bottle marked 'poison,' it is certain to disagree with you sooner or later."
—Lewis Carroll

MILKWEED

Milkweed is a good poisonous plant. Yes, really! Here's the thing—milkweed is the host plant for monarchs. What does this mean and why should you care? It means that monarch caterpillars *need* this plant in order to survive, and this is important since the monarch population has been plummeting! As gardeners, we can help by planting milkweed in our gardens. So even though the milky sap that runs through this plant's leaves can make you (and your pets) quite ill if you consume it, it's still a good perennial to have in your backyard.

DEADLY STATS

Common Name	Milkweed, common milkweed
Botanical Name	*Asclepias syriaca*
Zone	3 to 9
Height	2 to 5 feet
Spread	up to 1 foot
Flower Color	Pink, white
Light Needs	Full sun
Level of Toxicity	2
Toxic Parts	All parts of the plant because of the milky sap that runs through it

BE AWARE

If you or pets eat it, you might experience vomiting and nausea. If you cut a stem or leaf, this plant will give off a milky substance. Don't worry—it's not toxic to touch, but be sure to wash your hands after you handle it. And don't chomp on it.

DID YOU KNOW?

Why don't monarch caterpillars die from consuming milkweed leaves? They are pretty much immune to it, which makes for a great defense mechanism. Over the years, animals have learned to *not* eat monarchs and their caterpillars. Isn't nature both fascinating and cool?

THE BOTTOM LINE

Despite it being a bit irritable, you should still grow milkweed. The benefits to the monarch population far outweigh the risks.

LANTANA

Lantana is native to the Caribbean. Most gardeners grow it as an annual, but you might find it year-round in warm areas of California or Florida. This is a bloom that is like fine wine: it gets better with time. The small clusters of flowers usually start out as a soft, single color. Then, as the plant ages, they change color and deepen. Grow it in a sunny spot, and you'll love watching it thrive as some of your other blooms fade in the heat of the summer.

DEADLY STATS

Common Name	Lantana, red sage, wild sage, yellow sage
Botanical Name	*Lantana camara*
Zone	10 to 11
Height	up to 4 feet
Spread	up to 3 feet
Flower Color	Red, orange, yellow, purple, white, pink, bicolor
Light Needs	Full sun
Level of Toxicity	1
Toxic Parts	All parts

☠ BE AWARE

If animals eat this plant, they might experience vomiting, diarrhea, depression, and even liver failure.

❯THE BOTTOM LINE❯

It's probably fine if you can keep an eye on pets.

TOBACCO

POISONOUS PROFILE

If you've ever wanted to grow your own cigarettes, then you've probably looked into tobacco before. There are many different plant types in the nicotiana family, but the burley tobacco is the one used to make cigarettes. For those wanting to try it, you might have to grow it as an annual since it prefers warm weather. Of course, it's important to point out that this plant contains nicotine, which can be poisonous whether eaten, handled, or smoked. So think about that.

DEADLY STATS

Common Name	Tobacco, burley tobacco
Botanical Name	*Nicotiana*
Zone	8 to 11
Height	up to 4 feet
Spread	up to 3 feet
Flower Color	Pink, purple, white
Light Needs	Full sun
Level of Toxicity	2
Toxic Parts	All parts

BE AWARE

Years of smoking can cause death, but in its raw form, eating tobacco can cause convulsions and loss of motor control.

▶ THE BOTTOM LINE ▶

Don't encourage tobacco use or planting of any type. Skip this one.

BLEEDING HEART

Bleeding heart might be one of the cutest, most adorable flowers you can grow in the garden. In the spring, this plant produces tiny little flowers that are shaped like hearts. They're truly one of the most unique blooms you can find in the plant world. Many gardeners like this one because it's an early bloomer and it's fairly easy to grow in shade.

DEADLY STATS

Common Name	Bleeding heart
Botanical Name	*Dicentra spectabilis*
Zone	3 to 9
Height	up to 6 feet
Spread	up to 3 feet
Flower Color	Pink, white
Light Needs	Full sun to part shade
Level of Toxicity	1
Toxic Parts	All parts

BE AWARE

It contains alkaloids, which can be toxic to both pets and people. All parts of the plant can cause skin irritation, so you might want to handle with gloves when planting or transplanting.

THE BOTTOM LINE

It's almost too cute *not* to grow. Plus, if you have shade, it's a great option. It's probably fine to grow, but keep an eye on kids who might be curious about the blooms (and may put them in their mouths).

SNAKEROOT

This plant could also fit in the wildflowers chapter, and it's also considered a weed by many gardeners, but it's still one you might come across in backyards. It's easy to grow, does well in shade, and easily comes back year after year. Don't be tempted by this easy-to-grow plant, though. It's not actually all that great.

DEADLY STATS

Common Name	Snakeroot, white snakeroot
Botanical Name	*Ageratina altissima*
Zone	3 to 8
Height	up to 5 feet
Spread	up to 4 feet
Flower Color	White
Light Needs	Full sun to part shade
Level of Toxicity	2
Toxic Parts	All parts contain a toxin called tremetol, a type of poisonous and unsaturated alcohol.

☠ BE AWARE

This plant is a big concern for farmers, if and when cows eat it. It can enter their system, contaminating both the meat and the milk, which can then cause poisoning in humans (also called milk sickness).

❯ THE BOTTOM LINE ❯

It's pretty weedy overall, and not really a perennial you want in your garden year after year.

LARKSPUR

Many gardeners grow this as an annual, planting new seeds each year. However, it easily reseeds on its own, so it might not be necessary. Larkspur (pictured here) looks very similar to delphinium and was once included in the same genus, but it's separate now. The flowers put on quite a show from early spring to the middle of summer. Gardeners love it for the blue blooms, but you can now find it available in many other shades.

DEADLY STATS

Common Name	Larkspur
Botanical Name	*Consolida*
Zone	2 to 11
Height	up to 4 feet
Spread	up to 2 feet
Flower Color	Purple, blue, pink, white
Light Needs	Full sun
Level of Toxicity	2
Toxic Parts	All parts, especially the seeds

☠ BE AWARE

This plant is mostly a problem in prairies and open areas where animals graze. If they eat a lot of it, it'll cause weakness, nausea, muscle twitching, and even death.

▶ THE BOTTOM LINE

It's probably fine in backyards, but keep an eye out for it in pastures and other wild areas.

FOXGLOVE

This is a very popular garden plant with its tall and cascading bell-shaped flowers. It has some fun nicknames, including fairy bells and dead man's bells. (This is your hint that it is, in fact, deadly.) While it's rare that this plant can do a lot of harm, it is not one to mess around with because it can definitely lead to death. If you like the look of this plant and don't mind the risk associated with it, it's fairly easy to grow both in sun and part shade.

DEADLY STATS

Common Name	Foxglove, dead man's bells, fairy bells
Botanical Name	*Digitalis purpurea*
Zone	4 to 8
Height	up to 5 feet
Spread	up to 3 feet
Flower Color	Pink, white, purple
Light Needs	Full sun to part shade
Level of Toxicity	2
Toxic Parts	All parts

BE AWARE

When a human or animal eats this plant, the digestion of it can produce a substance called digitalis that affects heart muscles, which can, in turn, lead to a heart attack. You will see vomiting first, so seek medical attention immediately!

THE BOTTOM LINE

If you don't have pets that like to eat it, you should be okay growing this garden favorite.

JACK-IN-THE-PULPIT

This plant could also fit in the wildflower chapter. It's a common plant to see out in the wild and the shade of the woods, especially in spring. This is one of the reason gardeners love it—it grows well in shady areas. The plant is definitely known for its unusual shape. It has this tall spike (in technical terms it's called the *spadix* and in nontechnical terms it's called *the Jack*) with a sort of hood on top. It looks a bit like a tropical plant, but you can easily grow one in the shady areas of your garden. If you do, don't forget to water it a lot!

DEADLY STATS

Common Name	Jack-in-the-pulpit
Botanical Name	*Arisaema triphyllum*
Zone	4 to 9
Height	up to 2 feet
Spread	up to 2 feet
Flower Color	Tiny green and purple flowers
Light Needs	Part to full shade
Level of Toxicity	2
Toxic Parts	All parts

☠ BE AWARE

If you or an animal eat this raw, you'll know it right away because it causes severe mouth pain. You might see swelling of lips, tongue, and throat.

▶THE BOTTOM LINE◀

Don't try to collect or eat parts of this plant. Grow it for a cool shade perennial, but keep pets and kids away.

FLOWERING TOBACCO

POISONOUS PROFILE

Love hummingbirds? The flowering tobacco is like a secret weapon when it comes to attracting them. Often overlooked, this annual with star-shaped, tubular blooms is like a magnet to them. If you like fragrant flowers, then you'll reap some of the rewards, too. These are some of the best scented flowers you can buy, so take a deep breath when you're outside, and you're sure to get a whiff of pure sweetness. On sunny days, the blooms actually close up. This might seem counterintuitive, but it's guaranteed to make your garden more interesting!

DEADLY STATS

Common Name	Flowering tobacco, ornamental tobacco
Botanical Name	*Nicotiana alata*
Zone	10 to 11
Height	up to 5 feet
Spread	up to 2 feet
Flower Color	White, red, yellow, green, pink
Light Needs	Full sun to part shade
Level of Toxicity	2
Toxic Parts	All parts, especially the seeds, contain the poison nicotine.

BE AWARE

If pets eat this, you might notice signs of staggering, weakness, nausea, vomiting, and diarrhea.

❯ THE BOTTOM LINE ❯

Grow it—it's great for hummingbirds. Keep pets away, though!

BUTTERCUP

Love yellow flowers? This is one you might want to grow in your own backyard. This perennial is common in wildflower areas, and it especially loves wet or moist areas. So you might see this growing near a river, pond, or stream. While some gardeners consider this plant weedy, others love it because it's easy to grow and has great color. You decide!

DEADLY STATS

Common Name	Buttercup, tall buttercup, meadow buttercup
Botanical Name	*Ranunculus acris*
Zone	4 to 8
Height	up to 4 feet
Spread	up to 3 feet
Flower Color	Yellow
Light Needs	Full sun
Level of Toxicity	1
Toxic Parts	All parts, but especially during the height of flowering season

BE AWARE

If you have an animal that eats this during the height of the flower season, they might experience mouth inflammation, abdominal pain, and digestion problems.

THE BOTTOM LINE

Grow it in your garden if you want, but know that it can be a bit weedy. Keep it away from growing in meadows or pastures where livestock will be.

ANGEL'S TRUMPET

How can a plant with such a sweet name be dangerous? These are popular (and beautiful) plants that gardeners have been growing for centuries, but they are also some of the most deadly backyard plants. Most know this plant for its unique trumpet-shaped blooms. However, all parts of this plant can cause serious problems. Even handling this plant can cause skin irritation. So this is a "look but don't touch" plant. And unfortunately (spoiler alert!), it's not really a recommended backyard plant.

DEADLY STATS

Common Name	Angel's trumpet
Botanical Name	*Brugmansia* x *candida*
Zone	8 to 10
Height	up to 10 feet
Spread	up to 5 feet
Flower Color	White, yellow, pink, orange
Light Needs	Full sun
Level of Toxicity	3
Toxic Parts	All parts, including leaves, flowers, seeds, and roots

BE AWARE

If the elements of this plant enter the bloodstream, they might bring on symptoms of muscle weakness, dry mouth, rapid pulse, fever, and hallucinations. Other serious symptoms could be paralysis, convulsions, and death. The seed pods (which can look like fruit) have the most concentrated toxicity and are most dangerous.

THE BOTTOM LINE

They might be tempting, but they're best to avoid if you have kids or pets in your yard at all.

DAYLILY

Daylilies have the great grassy foliage of an ornamental grass while also producing beautiful and colorful blooms. While flowers only last for a day (hence the name), there almost always seems to be an endless supply of blooms because they really keep going all summer. It doesn't need much care at all. Plus, many gardeners consider them drought tolerant. You can get them in a huge range of colors.

DEADLY STATS

Common Name	Daylily
Botanical Name	*Hemerocallis*
Zone	3 to 9
Height	up to 3 feet
Spread	up to 3 feet
Flower Color	Nearly every color except blue
Light Needs	Full sun to part shade
Level of Toxicity	1
Toxic Parts	All parts can irritate cats

BE AWARE

This plant is particularly harmful to cats—it's been known to cause kidney problems. And it can give dogs an upset stomach.

THE BOTTOM LINE

Grow it! Daylilies are fantastic additions to backyards for the great foliage and blooms that last all summer.

HOSTA

Everyone seems to have areas in their yard that don't see much sun, and hostas are some of the best plants that will survive and thrive in those conditions. Hallelujah! Don't write off hostas as being boring or ordinary in any way. Sure, they've been around for years, but there are so many options available today. You can get all kinds of different leaf colors, shapes, patterns, and textures. Plus, many have a pretty great offshoot of flowers, too.

DEADLY STATS

Common Name	Hosta
Botanical Name	*Hosta*
Zone	3 to 8
Height	up to 4 feet
Spread	up to 6 feet
Flower Color	Grow for foliage with purple or white blooms
Light Needs	Sun to shade, depending on cultivar
Level of Toxicity	1
Toxic Parts	All parts

BE AWARE

If pets eat hostas, they might experience vomiting, diarrhea, or even depression.

❯THE BOTTOM LINE❯

Hostas are still a staple in most backyards. Keep an eye on pets when planting new hostas, but they should leave the plant alone during most of the season.

OPIUM POPPY

All garden poppies can be poisonous, but these are a little more dangerous because they contain opium. Yes, the same opium found in codeine, which can be a beneficial medicine to many. However, opium is also found in heroin, making it deadly to many, as well. Let's focus on the garden benefits for a moment, though. They are gorgeous plants with nectar-rich flowers that are attractive to bees. This is also the plant that gives us the poppy seeds we eat on many baked goods.

DEADLY STATS

Common Name	Poppy, opium poppy, breadseed poppy
Botanical Name	*Papaver somniferum*
Zone	5 to 9
Height	up to 4 feet
Spread	up to 3 feet
Flower Color	Red, white, coral, yellow, purple
Light Needs	Full sun
Level of Toxicity	3
Toxic Parts	All parts, but especially the stems, which when sliced open, produce a milky sap that opium is produced from

BE AWARE

Opium is used as pain suppressors and mood elevators. It might seem fun to grow your own opium poppies, but misuse can cause bloodroot poisoning and problems with the central nervous system, which can lead to death.

❯THE BOTTOM LINE❯

This isn't one to mess around with. Don't grow plants to harvest as your own drugs . . . ever.

SOLOMON'S SEAL

POISONOUS PROFILE

Once gardeners find out about Solomon's seal, they usually love it and grow it yearly. This plant looks a lot like hostas at first glance because of its rich, beautiful foliage. Also keep an eye out for the little blooms and berries that develop on the underside. Don't even think about eating those berries, though. You'll definitely regret it.

DEADLY STATS

Common Name	Solomon's seal
Botanical Name	*Polygonatum biflorum*
Zone	3 to 8
Height	up to 3 feet
Spread	up to 2 feet
Flower Color	Greenish white
Light Needs	Part to full shade
Level of Toxicity	1
Toxic Parts	All parts, but especially keep an eye out for the berries

☠ BE AWARE

You'd have to consume quite a bit to cause serious problems, but the plant and the berries could cause vomiting, nausea, and more.

▶ THE BOTTOM LINE ◀

This is a great option for shady areas, so plant away. Just keep kids and pets away from eating.

CHINESE LANTERN

Here's another unique plant, and gardeners definitely love unique! The round pods that form near the fruit of this plants are so cool looking! They are paper-like in texture, and definitely add interest to a container or flower display. However, anyone who has grown them knows how easily they can take over, making them a lot more annoying than cool. You might be tempted by these interesting plants, but there are definitely better options out there.

DEADLY STATS

Common Name	Chinese lantern
Botanical Name	*Physalis alkekengi*
Zone	2 to 9
Height	up to 3 feet
Spread	up to 3 feet
Flower Color	White flowers but known for the red papery "lanterns" that appear
Light Needs	Full sun to part shade
Level of Toxicity	2
Toxic Parts	Leaves, berries

BE AWARE

If the berries on this plant are ripe, they're edible. But if not, they can cause headache, vomiting, breathing problems, and numbness.

THE BOTTOM LINE

Stay away! This plant is aggressive, weedy, and potentially deadly. This is enough to put it in the "don't plant" category.

LUPINE

The entire lupine family of flowers are gorgeous backyard plants with somewhat rare blooms that gardeners are often after. They aren't big plants and they don't have big flowers, but they definitely make an impact in the garden with clusters of flowers on tall stalks. Lupine blooms in summer, and once you get it started, you'll look forward to it each year!

DEADLY STATS

Common Name	Lupine
Botanical Name	*Lupinus perennis*
Zone	3 to 8
Height	up to 2 feet
Spread	up to 2 feet
Flower Color	Blue, purple, white, and sometimes pink
Light Needs	Full sun to part shade
Level of Toxicity	1
Toxic Parts	Seeds

☠ BE AWARE

If you or pets eat the seeds of this plant, you might see signs of depression, slow heartbeat, and convulsions. These plants are most problematic if you have a dog or grazing animals that like to munch on a lot of plants.

THE BOTTOM LINE

Lupine makes a nice backyard garden plant. Keep an eye on your pets if they're around it, but it's a good addition.

AGAVE

POISONOUS PROFILE

The southwest is filled with this popular succulent, but you won't find it in cold areas unless a gardener is moving it indoors in winter or growing it as a houseplant. It's also known by the name century plant because legend says that it might live one hundred years before it blooms! In reality, it's more like ten or twenty years, but it's still worth noting. It does have gorgeous blooms, but you can't count on them.

DEADLY STATS

Common Name	Agave, century plant
Botanical Name	*Agave americana*
Zone	8 to 10
Height	up to 6 feet
Spread	up to 10 feet
Foliage	Green, succulent leaves
Light Needs	Full sun
Level of Toxicity	1
Toxic Parts	All parts contain a toxic sap.

BE AWARE

If your skin (or an animal's) comes into contact with the sap, it can cause terrible skin irritation. If eaten, you'll definitely notice digestive problems.

THE BOTTOM LINE

Be careful handling this plant, but you should otherwise be able to grow it without worry.

BABY'S BREATH

POISONOUS PROFILE

It's not native to the United States, but this plant is now making its way throughout the country. In fact, it's common to see it in wildflower seed mixes, too. It's a fun one to grow because the plants produce so many tiny white flowers, making it a great backdrop to a perennial bed or as cut flowers. Since it's been growing in popularity, there are a lot more options these days, so ask someone at your local garden center for a recommendation if you want to grow it!

DEADLY STATS

Common Name	Baby's breath
Botanical Name	*Gypsophila paniculata*
Zone	3 to 9
Height	up to 3 feet
Spread	up to 3 feet
Flower Color	White
Light Needs	Full sun
Level of Toxicity	1
Toxic Parts	All parts

BE AWARE

If pets eat this plant, it may not be life threatening, but it may cause vomiting, dermatitis, and upset stomachs.

❯THE BOTTOM LINE❯

Because it's a common addition to flower arrangements, it's just good to keep an eye on pets with cut flowers. Otherwise, feel free to grow it in your backyard without much concern.

FLAX

This is a small but mighty plant that is fun to grow in the backyard. You seriously just need to sprinkle the seeds in your garden, and they'll likely flourish from there! The blooms aren't very big, but they come in gorgeous bluish colors. Flax can take dry conditions and lots of different soil types. So if you want something easy, this just might be your new favorite plant! It should come back year after year, but if not, just sprinkle more seeds each year and grow it as an annual.

DEADLY STATS

Common Name	Flax
Botanical Name	*Linum perenne*
Zone	5 to 8
Height	up to 2 feet
Spread	up to 1 foot
Flower Color	Blue or purple
Light Needs	Full sun to part shade
Level of Toxicity	1
Toxic Parts	Seeds contain a form of cyanide

☠ BE AWARE

Flaxseed you get from the store is fine because it's been processed properly. However, the toxicity problem occurs when livestock eat the plant (and therefore the seeds) in the wild or if flaxseed is part of their food. Large doses could cause anxiety, dizziness, headaches, and vomiting.

▶ THE BOTTOM LINE ▶

Grow flax in your garden. It's one of those great plants that are *so* easy to grow!

YUCCA

You can get a little taste of the desert by planting yucca. It does well in poor or sandy soils, and it definitely is eye catching when growing in the garden. It has spiky green foliage that looks like it could be growing in the Southwest. Then in the summer, it will send off tall stalks of gorgeous, bell-shaped white flowers several feet into the air. Even after the blooms fade, you'll still have that spiky foliage to add some fun to your garden.

DEADLY STATS

Common Name	Yucca, Adam's needle, needle plant
Botanical Name	*Yucca filamentosa*
Zone	5 to 10
Height	4 to 8 feet
Spread	2 to 3 feet
Flower Color	Grown for its spiky green foliage and also shoots off-white blooms
Light Needs	Full sun
Level of Toxicity	1
Toxic Parts	All parts

BE AWARE

While it tends to be mild, still keep an eye on pets around this plant because it can cause vomiting, upset stomach, and diarrhea.

THE BOTTOM LINE

Grow it. It's a dramatic perennial that works well in many different spaces. The spiky nature of this plant keeps most pets away. You'll still want to be aware of it, though.

CARDINAL FLOWER

Cardinal flower is known among gardeners as a great plant for hummingbirds (they do love the color red). It's also a popular option for butterflies. This native perennial is a great one to get started in your garden. The flowers are bold and beautiful, and once you get this plant established, you'll have great blooms for many years to come.

DEADLY STATS

Common Name	Cardinal flower
Botanical Name	*Lobelia cardinalis*
Zone	3 to 9
Height	up to 4 feet
Spread	up to 2 feet
Flower Color	Mostly red, sometimes white or pink
Light Needs	Full sun to part shade
Level of Toxicity	1
Toxic Parts	All parts

BE AWARE

Pets who eat parts of this plant, especially in large quantities, might experience depression, vomiting, excess salivation, and abdominal pain.

THE BOTTOM LINE

It's still a good perennial for most backyards. Just keep an eye on pets and kids.

LILY-OF-THE-VALLEY

Lily-of-the-valley is popular plant among home gardeners because you can grow it as a ground cover. This means if you plant lily-of-the-valley in a small area of your garden, it can spread several feet in any and all directions in a few years. Of course, not everyone likes an aggressive plant. If you don't want it to spread, be sure to plant in a contained area (like a container or where there's a strong border around it). If you're going to grow it, keep an eye out in fall. This is when the plant can produce small reddish berries, which could look especially appealing to pets or small kids.

DEADLY STATS

Common Name	Lily-of-the-valley, lily of the valley
Botanical Name	*Convallaria majalis*
Zone	3 to 8
Height	up to 1 foot
Spread	up to 1 foot
Flower Color	Pink, white
Light Needs	Part shade to full shade
Level of Toxicity	3
Toxic Parts	All parts

BE AWARE

All parts of the plant contain harmful cardiac glycosides, which are especially concentrated in the underground roots and stems. This can cause nausea, dizziness, and in extreme cases, cardiac arrest.

THE BOTTOM LINE

Even though all parts of this plant are poisonous and it's a bit aggressive, this is still a perennial that many gardeners continue to grow. It pops up early in spring and lasts well into fall, so you can really get a lot of life out of it.

FOUR O'CLOCKS

There's so much to say about this plant. First off, many think of it as having edible flowers, so the fact that it's on a "toxic plants" list might surprise some. But it is true—it's better not to consume this plant. Even if there are times or parts that are okay to eat, you probably don't want to chance it! Most gardeners grow it as an annual, but some can grow it as a perennial. It has a bit of a tropical look to it, and it gets its name because the blooms don't come out until the afternoon—around the four o'clock hour! While you don't want to eat it, it's still a good annual and a perfect plant for containers!

DEADLY STATS

Common Name	Four o'clocks, marvel of Peru
Botanical Name	*Mirabilis jalapa*
Zone	9 to 11
Height	up to 3 feet
Spread	up to 3 feet
Flower Color	Pink, red, yellow, white, rose
Light Needs	Full sun to part shade
Level of Toxicity	1
Toxic Parts	All parts can have toxic elements.

BE AWARE

If ingested, you might see signs of nausea or vomiting. Some people even report problems with skin irritation after they handle four o'clocks.

THE BOTTOM LINE

Don't eat it. Just grow it for its beautiful flowers.

FRUITS & VEGGIES

"Perfection is beyond the reach of humankind, beyond the reach of magic. In every shining moment of happiness is that drop of poison: the knowledge that pain will come again. Be honest to those you love, show your pain. To suffer is as human as to breathe."
—Albus Dumbledore, *Harry Potter and the Cursed Child*

ASPARAGUS

Asparagus is one of those investment crops. It might take a year or two to get them established in your garden before they really produce, but once they do—wow! You can get a bountiful harvest for many, many years. Make sure you find a good, permanent area to grow your asparagus since it will come back year after year. It's not exactly easy to relocate. Once the crop is done for the season, let the foliage grow. It can get quite tall and give good height and color to your garden. It also makes a great background plant in the flower garden or a good screen.

DEADLY STATS

Common Name	Asparagus
Botanical Name	*Asparagus officinalis*
Height	up to 5 feet for most
Spread	up to 2 feet
Light Needs	Full sun to part shade
Level of Toxicity	1
Toxic Parts	The red berries, which come later in the season

BE AWARE

If asparagus isn't harvested and it continues to grow, it will produce small red berries, which can definitely be toxic. They can cause vomiting, nausea, and more.

THE BOTTOM LINE

Keep growing asparagus in your backyard. Just don't let it go past its prime and develop those little berries, especially if you have small kids or pets.

RHUBARB

Many gardeners consider rhubarb a perennial. Hardy in zones 3 to 8, rhubarb definitely deserves a spot in your flower bed, not just in your veggie garden. It's one of the earliest things to grow in spring and has beautiful green leaves and pinkish red stalks. Once you harvest and cook these stalks, you'll definitely want to try your hand at making a rhubarb pie (or rhubarb strawberry pie). Just stay away from the leaves, though. With more research, you should be able to find some ornamental ones that are not only pretty but edible, too!

DEADLY STATS

Common Name	Rhubarb
Botanical Name	*Rheum x cultorum*
Height	up to 3 feet
Spread	up to 4 feet
Light Needs	Full sun to part shade
Level of Toxicity	2
Toxic Parts	The leaves are most poisonous.

BE AWARE

The leaves contain something called oxalic acid, which can cause kidney failure in humans! Of course, you'd need a lot of leaves for this to happen, but it's still not a good idea to eat them.

THE BOTTOM LINE

This is still a good option for your garden, unless you have a pet that likes to munch away a *lot*.

POTATOES

Potatoes are poisonous? What? Don't freak out too much. This is still a good backyard veggie. You don't need much—just well-drained soil and consistent water. It's truly one of the easiest veggies to grow. Plus, you have so many great potato options. Big, small, purple, gold, white—there are plenty to choose from!

DEADLY STATS

Common Name	Potatoes
Botanical Name	*Solanum tuberosum*
Height	plants grow up to 3 feet
Spread	up to 3 feet
Light Needs	Full sun
Level of Toxicity	2
Toxic Parts	Leaves, stems, and sometimes the potato itself

BE AWARE

Both the stems and leaves of potatoes contain a poison called glycoalkaloid. This can actually be found in potatoes that turn green, so stay away if you notice this has occurred, especially if you're pregnant! Though rare, if you consume this in large quantities, it can cause weakness, coma, or even death.

❯ THE BOTTOM LINE ❯

Potatoes are a good option for your veggie garden.

TOMATOES

POISONOUS PROFILE

You just can't beat the flavor of a homegrown tomato, and in this day and age, you seriously have hundreds of varieties to choose from. Love heirlooms? You can get tomatoes in funky shapes and shades of purple, green, black, and orange. Looking to grow in containers? There are tons of options cultivated for pots and patios. Most tomato plants require about eight hours of sunlight a day, and they also need to be staked (or you can use a cage) so they don't flop over. You're not going to want to eat the leaves or stems, though. Yep, they definitely do more harm than good.

DEADLY STATS

Common Name	Tomatoes
Botanical Name	*Lycopersicon esculentum*
Height	up to 6 feet
Spread	up to 6 feet
Light Needs	Full sun
Level of Toxicity	2
Toxic Parts	Leaves, stems

BE AWARE

Like the potato, tomatoes also have the glycoalkaloid chemical. This can cause nervousness, upset stomach, or even be more serious in large quantities.

GREEN THUMB TIP

Tomatoes are one of those plants that a lot of gardeners like to start by seed indoors. Here's the biggest tip—don't start your seeds too soon. This way, they won't become "leggy" and die off before you get a chance to transplant them!

THE BOTTOM LINE

Grow tomatoes. They are delicious, relatively easy to grow, and there are so many awesome varieties to choose from.

CHERRIES

There's something romantic about having a cherry tree in your backyard. Imagine going outside in the summer and plucking off a few pieces of fruit to eat right there. So how in the world can cherries be poisonous? Is this something you need to worry about? The short answer? Not really. If you're looking for a fruit tree for your backyard, it's still a good candidate. Plus, the blooms in spring are gorgeous!

DEADLY STATS

Common Name	Cherry
Botanical Name	*Prunus avium or Prunus cerasus cultivars*
Height	most backyard trees are up to 15 feet
Spread	up to 15 feet
Light Needs	Full sun to part shade
Level of Toxicity	2
Toxic Parts	The seeds or pits of cherries contain a substance called cyanogenic glycosides, which can act as a form of cyanide.

☠ BE AWARE

If you accidentally swallow a cherry seed, you likely won't have to worry because it wouldn't be enough to do much harm. However, if you consumed a lot or if you chewed the seeds, thus releasing the substance, it could be pretty dangerous.

❭ THE BOTTOM LINE ❭

They are fine to grow and even eat, but make sure you and your children don't swallow the seeds.

KIDNEY BEANS

POISONOUS PROFILE

The kidney bean, a common food in chili and salad, got its name from its shape. It looks a lot like a human kidney! Like most beans, kidney beans are relatively easy to grow in the garden because you can grow straight from seed. For the most part, kidney beans aren't a problem, but they can be toxic in raw form, so it's important to know the basics before growing or eating them.

DEADLY STATS

Common Name	Kidney bean, red kidney bean
Botanical Name	*Phaseolus vulgaris*
Height	plants are up to 4 feet
Spread	up to 4 feet
Light Needs	Full sun
Level of Toxicity	1
Toxic Parts	The beans

☠ BE AWARE

Raw kidney beans contain a substance called phytohemagglutinin. If you don't soak these beans first, you could see signs of nausea, vomiting, and diarrhea. Other beans also contain this substance, but it's much higher in the red kidney bean. Cooked or canned beans are fine.

⟩ THE BOTTOM LINE ⟩

Like most beans, this one is a good option to grow.

MUSHROOMS

Do not eat a mushroom in the wild unless you know 100 percent and without a doubt that it's not poisonous. This cannot be stated enough. There have been too many accidents out there of people hunting for mushrooms out in the wild misidentifying them. This can cause serious harm, or even death, so you have to be careful. One of the most serious mushrooms you want to avoid is called death cap, which is the botanical name listed below. If you are interested in mushrooms and learning which ones are okay, consult an expert or a book on this specific topic.

DEADLY STATS

Common Name	Mushroom
Botanical Name	*Amanita phalloides*
Height	up to 6 inches
Spread	up to 6 inches
Light Needs	Full sun to full shade
Level of Toxicity	3
Toxic Parts	All parts

BE AWARE

Depending on the mushroom, you might see symptoms of just nausea, or you might see more serious symptoms like hallucinating, vomiting, and more.

THE BOTTOM LINE

Avoid wild mushrooms unless you really know what you're doing. It's too risky for those who don't or who are unsure.

ACKEE

The ackee tree is native to west Africa, but a lot of people now identify it with Jamaica, which is probably one of the few places you'd actually come across it, too. The ackee fruit is actually the national fruit of Jamaica. The large red, apple-like fruit looks unique. When it's allowed to ripen on its own, it will split, revealing the fruit inside, along with black seeds. However, if it doesn't ripen on its own, the results can be deadly.

DEADLY STATS

Common Name	Ackee, akee
Botanical Name	*Blighia sapida*
Height	tree grows up to 30 feet
Spread	up to 20 feet
Light Needs	Sun to part shade
Level of Toxicity	3
Toxic Parts	Many parts of the fruit, but especially the black seed

☠ BE AWARE

If you attempt to eat the fruit of this plant when it's not ripe, you will definitely become ill! It can lead to vomiting, coma, or even death in extreme cases. There's something in Jamaica called "Jamaican vomiting sickness," and this fruit is the reason.

▶ THE BOTTOM LINE ◀

Only eat it if you know it's safe—when it's ripe.

CASHEWS

The cashew is a fascinating tree. Native to Brazil and common in tropical areas, it actually produces fruit that look a lot like pears or apples. Then the cashew, which is actually the fruit's seed, comes out of the bottom! So you could say the cashew isn't even a nut at all. It's really just the seed of a fruit! The cashew itself isn't usually deadly, but it can be harmful in its raw form.

DEADLY STATS

Common Name	Cashew tree
Botanical Name	*Anacardium occidentale*
Height	most trees reach about 20 feet
Spread	up to 15 feet
Light Needs	Full sun
Level of Toxicity	1
Toxic Parts	The fruit and its seed (a.k.a the cashew) both contain urushiol, which is the same chemical in poison ivy.

☠ BE AWARE

If you come into contact with raw cashews or the fruit of a cashew tree, you could see irritation, much like you would with poison ivy. If you consume either raw, you might experience vomiting, nausea, and sickness.

▶ THE BOTTOM LINE ▶

You probably won't ever come into contact with a cashew tree or raw cashews because these grow in tropical regions. But if you do, it's best to avoid them!

SQUIRTING CUCUMBERS

This little perennial is definitely unique. The fruit on it looks like a fuzzy little cucumber, and when it's ripe, it will actually squirt out some liquid. . . . Some people say it's like a little explosion. It might seem fun to have this one growing in your backyard, but just say no. In areas where it's native, it's actually considered a weed, so you don't really want to get it started.

DEADLY STATS

Common Name	Squirting cucumber
Botanical Name	*Ecballium elaterium*
Height	up to 3 feet
Spread	up to 1 foot
Light Needs	Full sun
Level of Toxicity	2
Toxic Parts	All parts

☠ BE AWARE

The side effects of ingesting the squirting cucumber can include diarrhea, kidney problems, or it can even be lethal in large amounts.

⟩THE BOTTOM LINE⟩

While it's not a very common perennial, some people like it just because it's unique and different. So if you come across it, it's best to avoid.

RESOURCES

Here are some of our favorite books, websites, and organizations when it comes to poisonous plants and learning more about the great world of gardening.

Poison Control
Poison.org

ASPCA's Poisonous Plants List
Aspca.org/pet-care/animal-poison-control

Wicked Plants: The Weed That Kill Lincoln's Mother and Other Botanical Atrocities
By Amy Stewart

National Gardening Association
Garden.org

National Garden Bureau
Ngb.org

Cornell University's Home Gardening
Gardening.cornell.edu

Missouri Botanical Garden's Plant Finder
Missouribotanicalgarden.org/plantfinder

PLANT INDEX

ABOUT THE AUTHOR

© Tina Gregory

S tacy Tornio has been a gardener her entire life. She used to love and admire the flowers that both of her grandmothers grew in their gardens. She also remembers the words of warning her grandmothers and parents would give about eating wild berries or plants.

Stacy is the former editor of the national gardening magazine *Birds & Blooms*. She's also been a master gardener and a master naturalist and enjoys writing about gardening and plants for national websites and publications. She believes plants are fascinating—they can feed, heal, and, in some cases, even cause harm. But with a little education, they can be absolutely powerful.

You can learn more about Stacy or find her additional books on her website, destinationnature.com.